Here's to your success!
XO Melinda

Praise For
THE CONFIDENT COACH

If you're a coach, or you want to be one, this book will support you to kick ass in your coaching business. If you want to help more people get what they want, keep your life in balance and make good money in coaching, this is a must read. It's written by a coach who knows the soul of coaching, walks her talk and understands every roadblock coaches encounter...and how to blast through them!

JEANNA GABELLINI, master business coach
and author of *Rock Your Profits*

Melinda's wisdom is like the FUEL to stoke the flame of your coaching business... this book is a MUST READ for coaches!

SAGE LAVINE, *best-selling author & CEO Women Rocking Business*

There has never been a more important time for coaches to "turn pro" - showing up with confidence that they have the abilities (and the systems and structures) to help their clients powerfully, and deeply. And finally, Melinda Cohan has created the manual for taking that powerful step. Read it. Then read it again. Then implement it. Your future self will thank you, and so will your future clients!

DANNY INY, best-selling author of *Teach Your Gift* and *Effortless*

This is a powerful book. I recommend that everyone read it to help them achieve more success, help more people, and live the life they've always wanted. Melinda is amazing at taking the complicated and complex and making it simple and demystified.

You're going to get so much value from this book. I can't believe she's sharing all this amazing stuff in one easy to read, effortless, awesome book. I know you're going to love it. Enjoy!

CHRISTIAN MICKELSEN, #1 best-selling author of *Get Clients Today*
and creator of *Free Sessions That Sell*

Finally, business advice for coaches that shows you how to make building a coaching business fun rather than just some elusive future goal. And, if you don't think business is your forte, you may surprise yourself and fall in love with all things businessy."

MICHAEL PORT, *NY Times* & *WSJ* best-selling author of
Book Yourself Solid and *Steal the Show*

This is a true handbook to become a unstoppable coach, chock full new practices to implement immediately to thrive in these fast moving times. A must read for any current or aspiring coach who wants to succeed in the "Results Revolution Era".

MARGARET LYNCH, empowerment coach and best-selling author
of *Unblocked: A Revolutionary Approach to Tapping into your Chakra
Empowerment Energy to Reclaim Your Passion, Joy, and Confidence*

Melinda has taken the guesswork and overwhelm out of what it means to start, grow and launch your business. Everything you need is right here in The Confident Coach. Just follow her step-by-step guidance and watch your business grow.

BARBARA HUSON, author of *Rewire for Wealth: Three Steps Any Woman
Can Take to Program Her Brain for Financial Success*

Coaches, look no further! You have found your gentle, yet fierce guide, AND the step-by-step process to starting, building and scaling your business. Melinda takes you on the full adventure; from conquering your mindset that holds you hostage, through back-office necessities and all the marketing techniques you'll need to get started and or continue growing your business. All your "yes/buts" end here!

KATE STEINBACHER, co-founder of The Coaches Console

What I love about Melinda is her ability to break things down into a step-by-step process that does not overwhelm you and yet provides all the critical information to help you get started and excel as a coach.

Before I met Melinda, I was all over the place with marketing, email, website, follow-up, tracking, you name it, and not making the money or having the impact I knew I could. My business was a mess. I tried to piecemeal it together with no real plan, system, or idea of how I was going to make it all work. Through my time working with Melinda, she has helped me build a profitable and sustainable business.

TOM BRUSH, coach and CEO of Advancement Designs

I just read *The Confident Coach* by Melinda Cohan. She delivers a five-star guide and how to uplevel your coaching business with a boatload of action steps.

As a diversity and inclusion coach, I applaud Melinda for taking the initiative to become a more inclusive coach herself. Melinda provides real-world examples of how to make changes and bring awareness into your coaching business in the area of inclusivity. As a John Maxwell coach, speaker, and trainer, my mentor says, "a leader is someone who knows the way, shows the way, and goes the way." Leaders lead by example; Melinda is indeed leading by example.

The Power of Networking section alone is pure gold. I leaped with excitement while reading about a topic that is a weakness for me. Melinda provides easy, straightforward networking steps that can turn a novice into a networking ninja.

DR. MELINDA C. HILL, The John Maxwell Team

Melinda Cohan has a unique embodied genius that helps me navigate and grow beyond my blind spots in my coaching business. If you are ready to grow your impact in the world and to get paid abundantly for that impact, this is a must-read book.

MASTIN KIPP, best-selling author of Claim Your Power
and creator of Functional Life Coaching™

I've known Melinda for years – I've watched how she runs her own business and how she teaches coaches to start, launch and grow their businesses. In The Confident Coach she gives you the strategies, steps and systems for creating a thriving coaching business you feel fulfilled and gratified about. She teaches from experience and brings love and passion to the topic. I only wish this existed when I started my coaching practice 22 years ago. Working with Melinda will save you immeasurable amounts of time, energy and money.

RICH GERMAN, founder of the JV Insider Circle

If you want to build a successful coaching business you need 3 things – confidence, credibility and clients. In her book, The Confident Coach Melinda Cohan gives a complete roadmap to follow for each. This book is a must read for anybody who is just getting started with their coaching business.

JAMES MEL, co-founder of The Virtual Coach

A recognized leader in the coaching profession, Melinda Cohan turns her unparalleled wisdom, experience and dedication to the business of coaching into a step-by-step business-building guide filled with practical strategies, engaging stories, time-saving tips and helpful exercises to grow a thriving and sustainable coaching business filled with clients you love. The Confident Coach is a must-read!

MICHELLE SCHUBNEL, group coaching expert and founder of Coach & Grow R.I.C.H. Academy

The CONFIDENT COACH

BUILD A BUSINESS YOU LOVE,
Attract Ideal Clients & Make a Lasting Impact

MELINDA COHAN

ADVANCE REVIEW COPY

Uncorrected proof for limited distribution

Not for sale

MIRASEE PRESS

5750 Avenue Notre Dame de Grace
Montreal, Quebec
H4A 1M4, Canada
www.mirasee.com

Copyright © 2021 by Melinda Cohan

Paperback ISBN: 978-1-7373742-3-7
Hardback ISBN: 978-1-7373742-4-4
E-book ISBN: 978-1-7373742-5-1

1 3 5 7 9 10 8 6 4 2

To all the courageous coaches and
entrepreneurs starting a business.

And to *you*, the confident coach, for
letting your courage be just one degree louder
than your fears and doubts
so you can serve others and make an impact in this world.

Download the Audiobook + The Ultimate Coaching Business Success Tool Kit (for FREE)!

READ THIS FIRST

Just to say thank you for reading my book, I'd love to share the audiobook version PLUS the accompanying Ultimate Coaching Business Success Tool Kit, at no cost whatsoever. It's my gift to you. — *Melinda Cohan*

Go to **www.confident-coach.com/toolkit** to get it!

CONTENTS

FOREWORD

Choices and Challenges

Every day brings with it a new set of choices to make and challenges to overcome. These choices and challenges show up in every area of life and field of pursuit that matters to us, including work and business, love and relationships, and health and wellness. Some are small, about a particular moment in time (How will I respond to that email? Will I eat the brownie? Can I be the bigger person in this moment of conflict?) And some are big, about the trajectories of our lives, and the mark that we aspire to leave on the world (How will I handle this business setback? Can I face this illness with poise and grace? Can I get past the bad blood that has poisoned a once great connection?)

For us to show up the way we want to in the world and be the person that we strive to become, we have to get better at making these choices and meeting these challenges.

But how do we do it? One option is the brute force of trial and error, informed only by the operant conditioning of the natural consequences of our actions. Crash your skateboard enough times, and you'll learn to ride it safely. Make enough bad decisions at work, and you'll eventually notice the pattern and start making better ones. Blow up enough good relationships, and you'll eventually learn what pitfalls to avoid. So brute force is one option, but it's a slow, painful, and expensive way to learn.

The other option is to be supported by someone who has experience, expertise, and perspective that you need, who is invested enough in your success and growth to gently direct your attention to the most significant things in your situation—the small changes that can make a big difference as you tackle those choices and challenges. That person, of course, is a coach. Coaching has always been the surest path to faster and smoother growth. That's why the top performers in every field have always sought out coaches to support them. This is true of superstar athletes (Michael Phelps, Serena Williams), performers (Nicole Kidman, Hugh Jackman), business leaders (Eric Schmidt, Oprah Winfrey), and politicians (Alexandria Ocasio-Cortez, Bill Clinton), and it is also true of countless everyday people who want to do better in their careers, relationships, and lives.

Coaching is on the rise, and for good reason. In the last couple of years, the world has been turned upside down, shaken hard, and turned upside down again. We've faced wave upon wave of a global pandemic, along with the economic fallout from the shutdowns meant to contain its spread. The murder of George Floyd was the match that ignited the too-long-ignored powder keg of racial injustice in the United States and around the world. We've seen unprecedented environmental upheaval in the form of hurricanes, floods, and wildfires, to the point where it wouldn't be an exaggeration to say that much of the world has been aflame. And of course, there has been the widening political polarization that came with the 2020 American elections, culminating in literal insurrection at the nation's capital. So to say that we live in crazy times would be an enormous understatement! Our world has never been more challenging and uncertain than it is today, and so the stakes have never been higher for our ability to make better choices and face the challenges of our lives head-on.

So we turn to coaches for guidance and support, which they are willing and eager to provide. But coaching isn't just a matter of lending a listening ear and offering heartfelt advice. Coaching is a specialized skill that requires training, practice, and yes, also coaching to improve. And like every other disintermediated industry in our modern economy, it isn't enough for a coach to just be good at coaching either. For them to consistently and sustainably help the people who need their help, they need to build a successful business around their expertise. So while the rest of the world turns to coaches to support their growth, where do the coaches turn for the support that they need?

For nearly two decades now, the person that they've been fortunate to be able to turn to is Melinda Cohan. As s a coach to coaches, she's helped thousands of her clients to see blind spots, break through barriers, and build thriving coaching practices. As CEO of The Coaches Console, she's built a technology platform that has taken so many of the struggles coaches face off the table so that they can focus on doing what they were born to do: coaching. From her unique vantage point as the coach to coaches and the creator of the infrastructure that powers their businesses, Melinda has always had a special insight into where the coaching industry is and in what direction it was going. As a coach myself, who has had the privilege to call Melinda a colleague and friend for the better part of a decade, I've always appreciated her ideas and insights. That's why I am so excited that she has written this book.

Creating the business and life that we want all comes down to making good choices and facing challenges with poise and grace. As a coach, you help others to do that every single day. Finally, in this book, you'll find the guidance that you need to do the same.

—Danny Iny, Founder and CEO of Mirasee
Author of *Teach Your Gift*, *Effortless*, and *Online Courses*

INTRODUCTION

Coaching in a Complex World

In 2020, the COVID-19 pandemic affected billions, leading to business and school closures, job losses, increased relationship and family stresses…the list of challenges and complexities went on and on. The repercussions continue to surface, making people's lives even more complicated.

Long before COVID-19, we were already seeing increased activism, protests, and riots demanding radical transformations. The ripple effects of injustice gave rise to movements like Black Lives Matter and #MeToo, and we witnessed other political events that will affect us for years to come. These, and many other factors, combined to create an environment of complex debate and righteous outrage.

Now, people everywhere are looking for ways to transform the chaos so we can create a better future.

The Increasing Demand for Coaching

As life continues to get more complicated, people are being pushed by their challenges and fears to intentionally transform their lives. The trouble is that they don't know what to do or how to change, so they need a way to make sense of their situation and figure out their next steps.

When I say that our world is complex and chaotic, it reminds me of a challenge on one of my favorite reality TV shows. One of the challenges participants have to complete is walking through a maze. Under normal circumstances walking through a maze is complicated enough, but through trial and error people can typically find their way on their own. However, for the challenge on the reality show, the participant walks through the maze *while blindfolded*. The participant has help from a partner who supports them from the sidelines giving instructions and guidance. Without the partner's help, it would be extremely difficult to navigate the maze.

Now imagine walking through a maze while blindfolded *and the walls are moving*! This is where much of the world is right now, and it isn't an easy place to be. It's almost impossible to navigate this level of chaos without guidance and expertise. The scenario changes so rapidly that the only way to make progress is to take quick, decisive action, because if there's hesitation, the situation changes again, and the struggle continues.

This explains why the demand for good coaching is higher right now than ever before. Because of the global transition to more complex and chaotic situations, more people than ever in every niche need support to get results, take actions that matter, and take back control of their lives. And they want and need a coach to help them find their way through it all and reach their destination.

As coaches, *we* are the leaders people are turning to, to help them navigate their challenges and lives with purpose and create a future they desire—not just to survive, but to emerge from the chaos and thrive!

In the seventeen years I've spent working with thousands of coaches worldwide, I have never seen a better time to start coaching or accelerating your business's success than today. With the rise in people actively seeking out coaches, we're seeing unprecedented demand for our services. Coaches who've been struggling are beginning to thrive, and those who are already thriving are experiencing new growth. According to a study done by IBISWorld, the life coaching market alone was valued at $1 billion in 2020, while the business coaching market's value was close to $15 billion.

It's our responsibility to stay educated and build a strong business so we can confidently offer our services to others— and more importantly, to support and guide our clients and communities through their most challenging circumstances from a place of bold commitment and fierce love. But not everyone can deliver the kind of coaching that the market demands, or at least not everyone can do it well enough to succeed *and* make it a sustainable, profitable business while also creating a lifestyle they love.

Many coaches, new and experienced alike, struggle to get their business going and put themselves out there. This isn't because they're bad at coaching, and it isn't even a marketing or selling problem either. It's because they were never taught the *business knowledge* and *infrastructure* required to support them as coaches. So rather than being confident and feeling like "real" business owners, they feel overwhelmed and burdened by their business.

Feeling confident in your coaching business means having intentionally structured, organized, and streamlined systems backing how you market, enroll, and support your clients.

Being a great coach is one thing, but having a successful coaching business is very different. It takes a whole different mindset and skill set. That's why I'm glad this book is in your hands.

So many coaches ignore the *business* of coaching and cobble their back office together, hoping and praying that something will work and clients will magically hire them. But hoping and praying are not success strategies! Additionally, new coaches who do attempt to work on their business often jump straight into advanced strategies without first mastering (or optimizing) the basic building blocks of the structure they need in their business.

I have a friend who's a world champion in karate. Every year, Ricardo dedicates one whole month to practicing one single fundamental karate move—because without mastery of the basics, doing anything more advanced would be counterproductive. Trust me: if world champions need to master and optimize the basics before getting fancy, then so do you.

To consistently help clients means *first* mastering the fundamentals of business to ensure that you provide the best content, coaching, and systems to facilitate results for every client.

Don't overcomplicate things! Keep your coaching business organized and streamlined so that you're working smarter, not harder. Let it be simple.

The more intentional and the better defined your business systems and processes are for list building, converting, enrolling, supporting, payment processing, and other back-office activity, the more your business will run like a well-oiled machine.

This magic behind the scenes allows you to feel confident, leverage your time, and know that your systems and processes will bring everything necessary to support clients in achieving their desired transformations. The stronger your coaching business and the more confident you feel as a coach, the better your coaching will be and the better you'll be able to take advantage of opportunities as they arise.

Whether you're an experienced coach or you're just starting out, this book will guide you through proven techniques to build, launch, and grow a thriving coaching business that you can feel confident about and proud of—one that is authentic, is aligned with your natural skills, and delivers consistent transformation for your clients and a great lifestyle for you.

My clients often say, "I wish I knew this business stuff years ago, Melinda, when I first started."

Do you know the best time to start something? Yesterday. The next best? Now.

I believe it's our responsibility as coaches to build a better business so we can be better coaches and build a better world. The business-building adventure ahead of you will be exhilarating, challenging, and increasingly rewarding. I'm honored to be your guide.

HOW TO USE THIS BOOK

To give you the best reading experience, the best learning experience, and the best business outcomes from this book, here are a few suggestions and recommendations:

On your first reading, go through the chapters in the order in which they're written until you reach the end. (You don't have to read it all in one sitting! However fast or slow you choose to take it, your timing and pace is perfect.) Working through the book in order, page by page, will enable you to grasp the core concept without missing a step. That way, you'll create a solid foundation for your business. Every time you encounter a new idea or exercise, you'll be prepared to absorb the new knowledge quickly and easily based on what you've previously read.

DO THE WORK. When you come across a question or exercise in a book you're reading, you might be tempted to skip over it, or to just think about your answers instead of actually answering in precise detail. I get it. You want to save time and keep reading so you can learn more. But the questions and exercises are there to help you progress faster, not to slow you down! They're like building blocks and will make the future sections and exercises in the book easier to complete because of the momentum you'll build as you go. If you take the time to give each answer careful consideration and write down your answers so that you can refer back to them later, the better this book will work for you.

As your business evolves, you may want to dip into specific sections of the book repeatedly. Chapter 9, Technology and Your Coaching Business, is worth revisiting any time you're considering adding a new technology to your coaching business tool kit. Chapter 7, The Coaching Business Roadmap, is one you'll likely want to reread over and over again so that you can continually support and promote your business's growth and evolution. Chapter 8, Moving Farther Along the Roadmap, is the place to turn to when you want to uplevel your marketing impact and your enrollment conversations. And Chapter 14, Building Balance, is always there for you to support your spirit and help you avoid burnout.

At the very end of the book, you'll find a treasure trove of additional resources to help you pinpoint and implement the changes you want to experience in your coaching business. Explore as many of them as you like!

Chapter 1
THE RESULTS REVOLUTION

The Evolution of Coaching

Back in 2004, I scribbled the words that (unbeknownst to me at the time) would become my calling on the back of a napkin: *"Eliminate the burdens and distractions of coaches so they can live their God-given potential."*

I knew the more I could help coaches be successful in their businesses, the more people they'd coach, and the more we'd build a better world. And as the world around us changes dramatically, coaching is going through a new stage of evolution.

It is crucial to learn from the past and understand how coaching has evolved. Doing so provides insight into the new types of buyers emerging in the world today. Without this insight, your coaching business and the way you support your clients may be based on outdated approaches, leaving you struggling unnecessarily. Leveraging the gift of hindsight better positions you for the opportunities available in today's market. So let's look first at where we've come from as an industry, and then at where we're headed next.

The Information Age

Coaching surged into popularity in the early 1800s, helping the poor find new ways to earn money. But in the 1830s, the word *coach* first appeared in the academic world when the University of Oxford used it to describe a tutor. And in the lead-up to the 1924 Olympics (remember the movie *Chariots of Fire*?), athletes started to seek out coaches to help them perform better. Coaching then shifted into a very different model, supplying exclusive services to give elite, talented, and well-to-do individuals a greater advantage.

From there, the concept of coaching broadened to include coaching for business executives in the 1940s. In the 1960s, Dr. Milton Erickson's work in the field of psychology pushed coaching to become more present-focused and solution-focused for positive change. From there, personal and life coaching emerged in the 1980s and 1990s. Coaching became a high-status lifestyle choice for people privileged enough to afford it.

By the late 1990s, coaching was typically based on providing information and being a sounding board for the client, who felt reassured that they'd spoken to their coach and had the information they needed. Back in those days, it was the *information* someone gained that created a sense of success, not change. But the tide was turning.

The Experience Age

As the coaching industry expanded to more niches in the early 2000s, it was still primarily seen as either a solution for elite performance or as a luxury tool that only certain types of people used.

Clients began to expect more than just information and somebody to talk to. They wanted to be immersed in the whole experience of the transformation process. They expected not only informative coaching sessions and great content but also an engaging and fun experience while they were learning and growing.

It also became important to clients to connect with others on similar paths. Due to this demand, coaches began to create communities, connecting clients to other like-minded individuals so they weren't alone on their journeys.

While the coaching itself was still the primary focus throughout the early 2000s, the overall *experience* a client had when interacting with the coach, their services, and their business was the "product" that coaching clients would invest in.

The Results Revolution

According to a study by IBISWorld, the value of the US personal coaching market grew from $707 million in 2011 to beyond $1.5 billion in 2019. And with that growth, the industry began shifting into the next phase of coaching's evolution that we're currently in today: what I call the Results Revolution.

In this new era, coaching clients are no longer only the wealthiest and most privileged. The everyday person, of all ages, races, and cultures, also is seeking change in a complex world. Coaching has become part of the mainstream.

With this shift, having information and a great experience—whether the client achieves the change they wanted or not—no longer defines success. Clients have grown tired of investing their time and money without seeing tangible results. Plus, the newer type of client (the everyday person) doesn't have the luxury of making wasted investments. The negative consequences are too great for them to not care about results.

With the Results Revolution, client expectations have shifted to prioritize the *results* and *outcomes* of their coaching experience. Clients not only want great information with a great experience but now also demand results from their investment in the coaching process. As coaches, we must be able to identify the results we help our clients generate and explain how the coaching process facilitates that journey of transformation. And we have to leverage the necessary tools and resources in our businesses to deliver on those promises so our clients get results.

These client expectations benefit your clients, who will achieve greater results, and also benefits your business by generating more client success stories, thereby making marketing simpler, leading to more referrals and easily enrolling more clients.

A coaching business that can't help its clients create real, long-lasting change will sooner or later become unsustainable. But a coach whose business *proactively supports* genuine client transformation becomes unstoppable!

What the Market Needs from You Now

So how will you succeed in the Results Revolution era?

To help this new type of client overcome their complex situations and get results, you must first transform your coaching business. This book supports you in just that.

However, you need far more than an online booking tool, or a notepad and a list of generic coaching questions, to build a solid, smooth-running coaching practice that delivers transformative outcomes for your clients. You need consistent results.

Consistent results are the *only* way to activate the Cycle of Confidence that takes you from leads, to clients, to client success stories, which then drive referrals of new leads.

*The Cycle of Confidence: Getting more of your ideal
clients first requires delivering transformative results*

This cycle is what really accelerates your coaching business' growth and maturity (and revenue). It also makes your marketing easier, as you don't need to "sell" your services because your clients' results speak for themselves.

To start the Cycle of Confidence moving and keep it turning, your coaching business must deliver four key market needs.

Market Need #1: Exquisite Client Support

To support clients in getting consistent results, you must go beyond the hobbyist approach and the just-show-up-for-the-session approach. Coaching clients need us to deliver an unprecedented level of support, not only during their coaching session but also before, after, and between.

18

Before each session, clients need to prepare effectively to get the most out of it. To accomplish this, provide confidential, interactive online forms for your clients to complete before each session, linked within every appointment confirmation and reminder email for easy access, and organized securely in a secured, confidential online client portal.

After each session, clients must turn their breakthrough ideas into actionable items that build new habits. They need follow-up with a simple post-session form to create deeper accountability for faster transformation.

Between sessions, clients need just-in-time support when they hit an obstacle. A brief exchange of messages with you in a secured, confidential online client portal between sessions can help your client maintain momentum.

It's your duty to prepare yourself too. Coaches showing up for sessions without advance preparation used to be the norm, but now it's become a hallmark of a lazy coach who isn't keeping up with the times. You must devote time and focus to clearing your own mind; reviewing your client's previous sessions, goals, and progress; and preparing for the session.

Market Need #2: Connection and Community

Most clients invest in coaching to serve their urgent needs: to improve a relationship, to be more productive, to get through a transition. But what I've seen, in my own business and the businesses of the coaches we work with, is that clients ultimately *stay* for the community and connection—the experience of finding their people and no longer feeling alone. The world is craving a new kind of connection.

The addition of community to supplement coaching packages, programs, and courses provides collective learning. According to a study by R. Keith Sawyer, Ph.D., associate professor of education in Arts & Sciences at Washington University, learning within a community accelerates the process and is more effective than learning on an individual basis. If clients feel stuck, they can borrow courage and motivation from others in the community; when things are going great, they get to contribute by lending their own inspiration, courage, and support to others.

Coaches need to support clients within individual sessions as well as create a community in which clients connect with and support each other. Collaborative community is the magic that maintains momentum, and momentum is how your clients generate consistent action and reliable transformation!

Market Need #3: Online Accessibility and Security

Market need has shifted, and clients now have the expectation of online video sessions and virtual events. You have a definite advantage if you're comfortable using tools like Zoom. According to the International Coaching Federation

(ICF), 74 percent of coaches increased their use of video calls for coaching in 2020, and 84 percent said that their clients adapted well to using new technology. But 40 percent were not confident they had the technology to keep their clients' data confidential and safe online.

With increasing concerns about privacy for users, people now require new levels of security and control. Email and web-based documents may no longer be acceptable for sensitive information and communications since, under certain circumstances, they may not be reliable, confidential, or secure.

Working online with a smooth-running back-office system means that you can welcome your clients to a stress-free experience while making sure their confidential information is secure. Plus, delivering content, courses, events, and communities securely online can help you serve more people, in new ways that you otherwise wouldn't reach.

Market Need #4: Inclusivity and Equality

Coaching should be available to everybody who needs it. Be mindful of who is included and excluded by your business's messaging, marketing, and offerings, whether explicitly or implicitly. You may need to expand client avatars, update marketing messaging, widen business models, or simply reinvent current offers through a lens of inclusivity.

For example, for many years our client avatar at The Coaches Console was a woman aged 40 to 60. We didn't specifically think of her as white, but we also never thought of her as *not* white. This avatar described about 85 percent of our audience, so we catered our marketing toward that avatar. But with the awareness raising of the Black Lives Matter movement pointing out social injustice based on race, and a deep desire to serve all coaches wanting to have a successful coaching business, I began looking at our marketing through a more inclusive lens. I still have a lot to learn about inclusivity, equality, and equity. This will be something I continue to improve upon in our business.

One simple thing we did was to start including images within our sales pages, registration pages, content, and other resources that included every type of person we *already* had in our audience (all races, all ages, all genders…), and guess what? We attracted *more* clients and prospects of all types. One person even emailed me to say, "Thank you for including people like me. I can see myself being successful with your support." By becoming more intentional in making our online presence more inclusive and a more accurate reflection of the people actually in our audience, we're able to help even more people generate greater transformation in the world.

Today's market is driven by the desire of many clients to buy from businesses that are ethical and inclusive. Clients will make a point of seeking out businesses that are built on values of equality, respect, and inclusivity—which puts courageous, compassionate coaches like you on their short list.

As coaches, we must implement the systems and strategies to meet these current market demands so that we can generate the transformations needed to thrive and grow in this rapidly changing world.

Favorite Frames

While I was studying at the School of Womanly Arts, founder Regena Thomashauer taught me the importance of reflecting on and remembering the highlights of an experience. She had a tool for this called "favorite frames."

Since learning this exercise from her, it's something I do with all my clients at the end of a session. We wrap up by discussing favorite frames—the top takeaways, aha moments and insights that stood out the most. By identifying these, you deepen your commitment to applying them in your business.

Take a moment to digest what you've just read. Process what you've taken in so you can make room for even more. Below are some of my favorite frames to recap some of the key points in this chapter.

- Client expectations have shifted to focus on the *results* and *outcomes* of their coaching experience (the Results Revolution).

- You don't need to "sell" your services because your clients' results speak for themselves.

- To support clients in getting consistent results, go beyond the hobbyist approach to your coaching business.

- Community is the magic that maintains momentum.

- Clients will make a point of seeking out businesses that are built on values of equality, respect, and inclusivity.

Feel free to add your own favorite frames in the space below!

Chapter 2
GAINING A
NEW PERSPECTIVE

Why Coaching Is a Necessity

Coaching is now far more than a nice-to-have luxury, or a tool for the high-achieving elite to maintain their performance. It's become a vital necessity for the lives we're living and the situations and transitions we all face.

People are wondering what they can do to create change that matters. And all good coaches are asking themselves, "How can I help?"

The answer is, you can serve and support others to make positive progress. But it starts with *you* seeing your services as a necessity and no longer just a nice-to-have luxury.

Do *you* see coaching as a necessity? Until you do, no one will.

So ask yourself these questions.

Why are your services necessary in the niche you're serving? If your clients don't create the changes they seek, what are the negative implications in their lives?

For example, many relationships were strained by either constant closeness or long-term distance during the COVID-19 pandemic, making the services of relationship coaches more necessary than ever, because without help to relieve that strain, divorce (or worse, abuse) could be on the horizon. Many people's careers ended or changed dramatically during the pandemic, and they needed the help of career coaches. The same applies for health coaches, business coaches, life coaches, and all other types of coaches: your future clients are relying on you to see their need and act on it.

I asked myself this same question at the start of the pandemic: "What makes my service of supporting coaches and their businesses a necessity right now?" Coaches of every kind, in every region, needed urgent help to move their businesses forward through uncharted territory.

I knew that coaches could deliver powerful support, providing the hope and possibility people needed to navigate the chaos. Without the support of passionate, results-focused coaches, more relationships would fail, more abuse survivors would suffer, more people would not find new work, and more and more people would be lost in the dismay and devastation instead of improving their situations.

Coaches were at the crux of our world's recovery from the pandemic and other global issues but to make it happen, those coaches needed to feel prepared and confident to put themselves out there! Coaches without a strong business back office struggled to step up to the new demand and struggled to facilitate change. Coaches without confidence in their businesses were quicker to give up on their dreams and started believing they should just close up shop. My answer was clear: to transform the world, coaches needed me to help them strengthen and systematize their coaching businesses so they could feel confident and coach more people.

Coaches needed support so that their courage was one degree louder than their fear. Confident coaches stepped up in big ways to support people through deep challenges and deep changes. Understanding what made my services a necessity meant that my *why* took on a larger meaning, and I was clear in the part I played in it. It drove me in the midst of uncertainty to take imperfect action and do whatever was necessary for me to put my services out there. Answering this question for your own coaching business will do the same for you.

What are the new challenges and urgent needs your clients are facing today that they weren't facing a year or six months ago?

When you can identify those new, urgent needs, you can adjust what you offer. You can modify your messaging, implement new material and content, highlight existing resources in your offers, create new workshops, and collaborate with new partners. You can even create new offers or pivot existing offers to address and serve your clients right where they are with what they need most.

What would your coaching offer need to look like to help your ideal clients meet their current and urgent challenges and needs?

Your offer is the way you package your services, courses, or programs that will help people get the results they want (and that you're promising). Consider what your offer could include, exclude, or make use of to best support your clients in their current states.

Would you continue to offer the same packages, programs, and services? Would you create something new? Would you relaunch an old program that's now relevant again?

The more you reflect on and answer these questions, the more you can see how vital your services are. And once you know your answers, it naturally becomes easier to set aside your own fears and doubts in the interest of serving those in need.

This new perspective is your chance to take charge of your own coaching business and to help others generate the transformations they desperately need.

The Power of Community

Starting your own business can be one of the hardest things you'll ever do. It can also be one of the most rewarding. Often new coaches mistakenly believe success is created from an isolated perspective, that they must figure it all out by themselves. This perspective must be shifted for sustainable success to be possible.

Isolation is the number one enemy of success.

Coaches frequently feel like they should know exactly what they're doing all of the time and that they mustn't show any uncertainty when it comes to their coaching business. And this fear-based mindset leads them to disappear, disengage, and disconnect when their doubts and villains start to get the better of them. The problem with that approach is that when you're isolated, you can't leverage the wisdom of those who've been on the same journey. When you're isolated, you don't know what you don't know, and in trying to figure things out in isolation, you can learn only through the hard and expensive path of trial and error.

The antidote is to be connected in a conscious community of like-minded and like-spirited people. That's where growth and opportunity are waiting! Community has a significant impact on your momentum, progress, and success.

When you're surrounded by a community of people who are part of and witness your journey with you, they can reflect and reframe what they've observed, and you can see yourself and your situation through a new lens. Your "normal" might be someone else's aha moment! So when you give another person the privilege of witnessing you and you hear their excitement or their aha moments, you realize the wisdom, skill, and experience you possess. Being witnessed *by* others within a community means you're stepping out in transparency and vulnerability in a safe space, and it's yet another way to cultivate your courage and confidence to take the simple steps—and also the bold, brave steps—your business needs you to take.

Being witnessed means that you know your colleagues have your back. The community acts as your safety net that won't let you fall down without catching you and propelling you back up again, giving you the strength and resilience to keep going. It's easier to try new things and learn from your efforts with collective support and encouragement.

Community transforms your perspective. I love to ski not just because the downhill experience is exhilarating but also because the perspective I gain each time I go to the top of a mountain is amazing. From the top, I can see things that I can't when I'm skiing down the slopes.

One of the reasons I'm in a mastermind group is because connecting with that community of colleagues and confidants gives me a fresh high-altitude view on my business. As my friend and mentor Jeff Walker said in our mastermind group, "We help each other get perspective." And I don't approach this through a lens of comparison or competition but rather of curiosity, clarity, or confirmation. My colleagues in the mastermind community help and inspire me to step more boldly into my business.

Just in case you're not convinced that a supportive community is a *necessity*, let me share the story of how community gave me the power to break boards with my bare hands.

The facilitator at the first coaching retreat I attended, back in the early 2000s, told the hundreds of attendees that we were all going to do a bad-ass martial arts move. We were going to break one-inch-thick wooden boards with our bare hands (for real!).

"Yeah, right," I thought to myself. I had zero experience in martial arts beyond watching The Karate Kid, and I'm a petite woman with normal upper body strength for my size. To be honest, I thought the facilitator was full of crap in promising us martial arts superpowers! I figured most of us wouldn't be able to do what he expected.

Then he said from the stage: "Everyone *will* do this. Everyone. I've been leading this retreat for years and there hasn't, not once, ever been a time where not everyone did this. I know you'll do it. You don't have to believe it. I already know, so borrow my courage and belief until you find your own."

That thought—"borrow my courage and belief"—hit me like a ton of bricks. I figured, heck, if he's so confident that I'll do it, then clearly he knows something that I don't!

He had the experience to know what was possible. He had the confidence that we could all achieve it. People who had attended his retreats before knew that we could do it, too, and they were wildly cheering us newbies on.

So I borrowed his courage. I had no idea how I'd do it, but I trusted, followed his lead, and *did it*! What was even cooler was that once I had that visceral experience under my belt, I was able to join the crowd in cheering others on from a whole new perspective, because I now *embodied* the confidence they needed.

I still have the inch-thick board I broke with my bare hand to remind me of the true power of community. And ever since that day, I've worked to help cultivate and facilitate connection and collaboration in conscious community as part of every coach's recipe for success—for their business and for their clients.

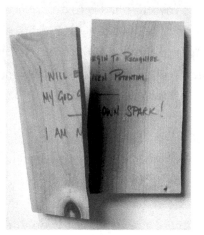

The power of community: With trust, support, and confidence (even if it's borrowed), you can do ANYTHING.

Ask yourself the following questions when you want to form or join a community. What communities do you and your coaching business have to support you? Where can you borrow a little courage when you need it? What communities provide a safe place where you can be transparent and vulnerable for optimal growth and impact?

But it can't just be *any* community. It has to be the right community for *you.*

My friend and mentor, Barbara Stanny Huson, taught me that community is not merely about gathering people together; it's about intentionally cultivating the specific type of community you want. You've heard some variation on the saying that we are the sum of the people closest to us, right? Quantity does matter, but quality matters much more!

In her book *Overcoming Underearning*, Barbara explains that there are five types of people you definitely want to have around you:

- True Believers: those who believe in you no matter what, even when you're facedown in the mud and all hope seems lost.

- Confidants and Colleagues: those trusted friends who always have your back and will take a stand for you.

- Way Showers: those who have already traveled the same path you're on and can show you the way.

- Messengers: those who share information that's necessary for you to continue the journey.

- Naysayers: those who don't think you can do it.

While it is harmful to hang around naysayers, I have personally found there can also be special circumstances where you may actually want them around—just at a very intentional and safe distance—because naysayers telling us we can't do something often motivates us to take on the challenge!

My dad, my greatest hero and a true believer, became my biggest naysayer for a brief time in one gut-wrenching moment early in my coaching career. We were having lunch together and I was talking to him about my business's early financial struggles. And he, as only a dad can do, tilted his glasses to the tip of his nose, peered over the top of the rims and said to me, "Melinda, it's simple. Your outgo is more than your income. You can't do this; you just need to get a job."

Those words felt like a knife in my heart slicing out my dreams. Of course my father meant what he said from a place of deep love, in support of making sure I could take care of myself financially *while pursuing my dreams*, but I couldn't hear that until the gift of hindsight had kicked in. All I heard at the time was that my dad didn't believe in me and thought I should give up.

So I stood up from the table, spat a few choice swear words that a minister's daughter should never say to her dad, and basically told him to "watch this!" In the coming months, I made darn sure my business was solid so there would be no way I would fail and have to get a job.

I created structures to support my work and support my clients so that I could over-deliver. I put mechanisms in place to grow my list of leads and prospects steadily, not just by one or two here and there. While most of my colleagues were focusing on the latest marketing fad, I was focusing on the back end of my business being so organized, stream-lined, and automated that it didn't require much of my time to handle it all. And because of that solid back end, when I did start marketing, it was like a machine of steady prospects, strategic referrals, and eager new clients!

A few months later, I had a full practice with eighteen paying clients and raving fans, who would refer new clients to me in the months and years to come, all because my dad shook up my passion with his loving advice. When it felt like he was a naysayer, he actually became my greatest motivator too. It was the first time I felt like a real business owner. And because of that single moment in history, because I stepped up to the challenge, my business has grown beyond the seven-figure mark and I'm supporting thousands of other coaches aiming to reach their own financial goal. It's thanks to my dad's momentary nay-saying that you're here reading this book!

If you've been used to working alone, or with limited support, then consider joining a group or a mastermind group in which the community is your most valuable resource.

Favorite Frames

Take a moment to digest what you've just read. Process what you've taken in so you can make room for even more. Below are some of my favorite frames to recap some of the key points in this chapter.

- If *you* don't see your coaching services as a necessity, nobody else will either.

- Your courage just needs to be one degree louder than your fear.

- Take imperfect action.

- Isolation is the number one enemy of success.

- Community acts as your safety net, giving you the confidence and resilience to keep going.

- Naysayers telling us we can't do something often motivates us to take on the challenge.

Feel free to add your own favorite frames in the space below!

Chapter 3
THE ENTREPRENEURIAL VILLAIN

The Perfect Enemy

While isolation is the number one enemy of success for entrepreneurs, perfectionism ranks right up there with it. New coaches often have the belief that everything has to be just right. If they feel it isn't just right, they won't move forward because they believe they'll fail.

Their website has to be perfect. Their free resources have to be the best. Their campaign has to be just right. Something always needs just one more tweak or one more edit. This procrastination could go on forever.

I'm a recovering perfectionist myself, so my first thought was that "I'm not the only one! Thank God!"

Working with coaches year after year, I began to notice how this pattern of perfectionism held coaches back, kept them playing small, and prevented them from getting clients. I started to notice it so frequently that I began to study our clients as they made their way through our coaching programs. Interestingly enough, I discovered that this pattern was a common response when someone stepped out of their comfort zone and took a leap toward their dreams. It's a natural human dynamic; we just can't afford to get stuck in it.

For the sake of clarity, I'm not referring to people who simply hold themselves to high standards of excellence. I absolutely believe in that approach and guide my team accordingly. But there's a different energy involved: behind high standards of excellence there's an energy of courage, while behind perfectionism there's an energy of fear.

I wanted to make it easy for coaches to identify this fear-driven pattern. I sat down with Kate, my business partner and the Queen of Fun, and we turned this pattern into a character: an entrepreneurial villain named Perfect Portia. When this villain takes over, you find yourself making countless never-ending revisions, second-guessing yourself, and experiencing analysis paralysis—anything to keep you from implementing and moving forward.

Perfectionism is a symptom of self-doubt. This fear-based busywork is one of the many villains that try to sneak in and sabotage your efforts. Once you let that fear mindset rule your business, you're losing.

Embracing Your Superpower

So how do you cultivate a courageous mindset in the face of your perfectionist fears? Meet your superpower, Dr. Richard Research. When you embrace the qualities of this superpower, you can feel confident about moving forward and generating rapid results.

From this perspective, you approach every project with the mindset that *it's all research*. You're curious about what you can learn as you create and implement. You know that with implementation comes feedback and data that will inform the best way to proceed. You don't freeze when it comes to taking action, because you've given yourself permission to make mistakes and learn from them. And you're able to quickly make adjustments, optimize, and maintain momentum.

We get stuck in perfectionism when we fail to see the totality of this research-focused path to results. Entrepreneurs mistakenly focus only on the learning. Without seeing the rest, implementation can feel scary, and self-doubt creeps in because if something doesn't work as planned, it feels like all or nothing; failure is the end.

However, when you know in advance that with each piece of learning and each step of implementation you will *also* research the results, debrief the situation, make adjustments, and do things differently for quick course corrections, you can commit to taking imperfect action for faster growth and rapid results.

The first step is to understand "failure" as a welcome part of the process; it's all research. When you fall down, there's no need to take it personally. You get back up, learn, and keep going. What I love about this superpower is that it's not that you win or lose, but as my good friend Susan Garrett, multi World Champion of dog agility, taught me, you *win* or you *learn*.

One of my favorite quotes comes from Michael Jordan:

> "I've missed more than nine thousand shots in my career. I've lost almost three hundred games. Twenty-six times, I've been trusted to take the winning game shot and missed. I've failed over and over and over again in my life. And that is why I succeed.

The following are additional quotes that demonstrate the benefits of failing:

> "Just because you fail once doesn't mean you're gonna fail at everything." (Marilyn Monroe)

> "Results! Why, man, I have gotten a lot of results. I know several thousand things that won't work." (Thomas Edison)

> "You may encounter many defeats, but you must not be defeated. In fact, it may be necessary to

encounter the defeats, so you can know who you are." (Maya Angelou)

"Everyone falls down. Getting up is how you learn to walk." (Walt Disney)

When I learned to embrace these quotes, my perfectionist tendencies shifted to holding high standards being driven by my passion rather than fear. I could focus more on my clients and less on me. Vulnerability and transparency as well as integrity are among my top values. As I began to move forward in the midst of mistakes—while being vulnerable enough to admit them, being transparent enough to ask for help, and having enough integrity to correct them— I stopped confusing professionalism with perfectionism. In those moments I made mistakes, I would receive responses from my clients and prospects saying things like "I'm so glad to know you're human; it makes me feel like having my own business is possible for me too."

Muhammad Ali was quoted after he lost a fight against Joe Frazier, saying, "It's a good feeling to lose. The people that follow you are going to lose too. You got to set an example for how to lose." This way they can see how I lose." I love that quote. It gave me permission to make mistakes, be vulnerable, make adjustments, and keep going with my integrity intact, modeling for my clients to do the same.

Learning doesn't happen in a vacuum, especially when we're talking about interacting with and supporting other human beings. We can know only so much, and then we have to learn from their insights and their responses. We observe, question, and learn to the best of our abilities; we research what we need to know, and at some point, all we can do is implement for results.

Take your lead magnet as an example (the free download resource you offer in your business in exchange for a person's contact information). Once you've studied what makes an effective lead magnet that provides great value, researched what your market needs are, and you've implemented everything to the best of your ability, the next step (not the final step, just the next step) is to put it out there, let others experience it, and then get their feedback. The data from this is priceless and vital for every entrepreneur. The same is true for everything else you put into the world, such as your coaching packages, the courses you build, and the campaigns you launch.

But the most powerful step in the process is when you do a debrief, which is when you review the situation and learn from it.

The Power Is in the Debrief

I learned from Jeff Walker that the debrief is where the power lies. I've come to understand through my own experience that the debrief turns every potential failure into opportunities and possibilities.

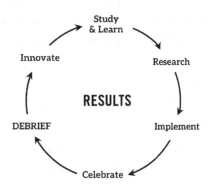

The Debrief: Make it part of every project cycle

After you implement and execute any project in your coaching business, ask yourself (and your team, if you have one) these three powerful debrief questions:

1. What went well?
2. What didn't go well?
3. What will I do differently next time?

The sooner you do the work of the debrief, the sooner you can learn from your experiences and implement the "do differently" ideas to optimize your results. Without this step, you risk getting stuck in failure-focused mode and grinding to a halt entirely!

Don't let Perfect Portia sabotage your efforts. Adopt Dr. Richard Research's spirit of curiosity and willingness with the mantra that "everything is research." When I adopted this spirit and started to debrief everything, asking myself these three questions, it was a game changer for my business *and* my life!

The debrief is how Michael Jordan has "failed" so often and is still considered the greatest basketball player of all time. And it's how you optimize your marketing, programs, campaigns, pricing, and every other part of your coaching business.

Favorite Frames

Take a moment to digest what you've just read. Process what you've taken in so you can make room for even more. Below are some of my favorite frames to recap some of the key points in this chapter.

- High standards of excellence come from courage; perfectionism comes from fear and self-doubt.
- Approach every project with the mindset that *it's all research*.
- Understand "failure" as a welcome and important part of the process.
- The debrief turns every potential failure into opportunities and possibilities.

Feel free to add your own favorite frames in the space below!

Chapter 4
SETTING YOURSELF UP FOR SUCCESS

Cultivating Your Work Environment

The space you work in supports your daily activities and energy (or not). In my pre-coaching life, I was an interior designer working with corporate clients. I used to study their teams and workspaces, then help them create the workflow efficiencies required to accomplish their corporate goals. Finally, I would design the work environment to support those workflow efficiencies so everyone could do their best work—because the space itself was conducive to it.

If you're working in a cluttered, disorganized space, then your energy and the quality of your work will also be cluttered and disorganized; distractions will be easy, and you'll fall prey to the "shiny object syndrome." That forces you to work harder for less progress, so by trying to operate in that environment, you're setting yourself up for overwhelm and failure. Instead, take some time to create a space that is inspiring, is a joy to be in, and supports the work you need to accomplish.

It doesn't have to be fancy or elaborate, just clear, organized, and efficient. In the early days of my coaching business, my workspace was a small sofa table, just twelve inches by thirty-six inches. I had my laptop, my mobile filing cabinet, my desk chair, and a good lamp. That's it. Sometimes I'd work from my sofa, other times at the dining room table. But the space I was claiming as my workspace was always clear, organized, and efficient.

Whenever I want to uplevel my business, I start by re-arranging or re-creating my office so that it has a new energy and is set up in a way that is conducive to my new goals becoming reality. When I wanted to cross over the seven-figure mark, I looked around and realized my office didn't *feel* like the office of a million-dollar business owner to me. So I spent a weekend rearranging and working with what I already had in my office and in my house, and I reinvented the space so that it felt like I was *already* the owner of a million-dollar business! That energy and intention paved the way, creating the container that made it possible for me to show up and work like the owner of a million-dollar business I was about to become.

Another good way to set your energy and intention in preparation for great work is to dress for work, even if—*especially* if!—you work from home. The attention you pay to how you dress for "going to work" makes a difference in your mind, attitude, and energy. If you feel casual, you might be more likely to do casual work. If you feel smart, confident, and professional, you'll work that way, too. So, dress for work! It really is that simple. You put on the clothes that match the job of a kick-ass coaching business owner, and you'll show up as that kick-ass coach.

Managing Time

A common misstep for entrepreneurs is what I call "extreme multitasking," which is when you're doing *everything* in your business, working ten- to twelve-hour days just to keep up, and you're still left wondering how you're going to get it all done.

Time is a finite resource. We all get the same amount of it, and it's your most valuable commodity. In the early phases of your business, when you often have limited financial resources, you try to do everything yourself. It's an impossible goal! If you keep up this extreme multitasking for too long, you'll burn out, so you need to manage your time effectively, which means you need to manage your boundaries and priorities.

One of the enticing things about working from home is the idea that you can set your own hours and be as flexible as you like, which, for some coaches, swiftly mutates into setting no fixed hours at all. Because entrepreneurs, and coaches in particular, are often passionate about the work they do, they may barely think of it as work or as a separate thing from the rest of their lives. While that's a blessing, it's also a curse—our passion can take over and before we know it, we're working at all hours, at any place, at any time, and it's our own quality of life and close personal relationships that suffer.

This is an issue of boundaries; without solid boundaries between your personal time and your business time, everything blurs together. That's a slippery slope, and if you don't stop the slide, one day you'll find yourself answering client emails at the kitchen counter while eating dry cereal with your bare hands at two in the morning!

Even if your commute involves walking only from the couch to the table, or from one room to another, set up your environment to be conducive to the work, and set your office hours likewise.

With extreme multitasking, everything can feel urgent. This is an issue of priorities. It's easy to have a to-do list that's several pages long. While those things must get done, our brains can focus on only one task at a time. Studies have shown that when our brain switches back and forth between tasks, we become less efficient, getting less done while making more mistakes.

I have found that when I can identify and focus on completing the top three tasks from my long list of to-dos, I actually get more done than if I try to focus on more than three at the same time. This approach takes a little thought to prepare in advance, so here's a short exercise to help you plan it out:

- At what time will you start your day and "go to work" in your designated office area?

- At what time will you finish work and leave your office environment to "go home" for the rest of the day?

- How will you set the boundaries of your office hours for others and remind them of those boundaries at the right moment (in other words, just *before* they decide to interrupt your prime in-the-zone time)?

- At the end of your workday, identify the top three things you'll focus on the next day. What materials do you need to easily complete those tasks? Get them prepared so that when you begin work the next day, you'll be equipped, focused, and ready to dive in.

The Rule of the Four Ds

To help you implement for success and work smarter, not harder, I want to share with you the Rule of the Four Ds. This quick and easy decision-making tool will help you figure out what to do with each of the tasks you find on your plate. Applying this technique in your business will save you time, effort, and money.

The Four Ds are *dump* it, *duplicate* it, *delegate* it, or *do* it. When you find yourself doing something that is not necessary for your business goals, *dump it*! If you're scrolling endlessly through Facebook or Instagram and you know it's a distraction and holding you back from doing something more productive, just stop!

A lot of the tasks on your epic to-do list are necessary and essential, like sending your welcome packet to a new client after they sign up. But if these are repetitive tasks, then you can *duplicate it* (and by that, I mean automate it) by using technology to automatically send the correct items to the correct people, at the correct moment. You remove yourself from the task, but it still gets done.

For tasks that are certainly necessary, but not so essential—and that can't easily be duplicated—start getting used to the idea that instead of doing it all yourself, a way to work smarter is to *delegate it*! Give these tasks to someone who will do the work faster, better, more easily, and/or more gladly than you. Start by outsourcing the $15/hour tasks, then the $25/hour and $50/hour tasks, so you can focus on revenue-generating activities.

And finally, you're left with only the tasks that are in your zone of genius and genuinely need to be done by *you*. I'm referring to the higher level, revenue-generating work in your business and the deep, results-generating work of coaching. For this type of work, you need to be the one to *do it*!

Being Prepared in Advance

"When preparedness meets opportunity, success is inevitable."
—Melinda Cohan (yep, I just quoted myself)

I admit, being prepared in advance is not a new idea. And you might wonder, is there really any other way to prepare?

Yes. Yes, there is. There are multiple ways to prepare badly, and I see them far too often. That's why I included a section about it in this book!

Don't fool yourself into thinking that preparation can be crammed in at the last minute—that's just procrastination and panic. To prepare for anything important means intentionally giving yourself time to think through your choices and their implications so that you can create the ideal strategy, and then giving yourself even more time to figure out the step-by-step actions to execute and test that strategy. Procrastination and panic create stress and adrenaline, which can lead to burnout if you're not careful. On the other hand, preparation and intentional planning elicit endorphins and other feel-good chemicals, allowing you to enjoy the process and not be depleted by it. This process is crucial to your success, so work backward in your calendar from whatever deadlines you've set, and block out enough time to complete your preparations long before those dates.

Real preparation requires planning *and implementing* systems in advance so that when your moment comes, you're ready to do your best.

You might not know this, but when I'm not working with our clients at The Coaches Console, my husband, Dave, and I organize ski and adventure trips for groups of twenty to fifty people. We're creating the adventure of a lifetime for participants—these trips are usually "bucket list" items—so it's important for them to have a great experience and create unforgettable memories they'll treasure for the rest of their lives. Lack of organization, details not being handled, and time being spent fixing or correcting things can only detract from the experience and turn those pleasant memories into nightmares.

When Dave and I think through of all the details in advance, and prepare for them to the best of our ability, it creates the best experience possible. But it takes foresight and paying attention to every detail of both the plan and its implementation. The more details we can pay attention to, the more fun everyone has, even us as the trip leaders. The same is true in your business.

When you plan and prepare in advance for what a client will experience in your program, at your event, within your marketing, as a student in your course, and so on, and you address every detail with attention and intention, then you create the best experience possible—setting your clients up for success and making sure they have fun while they're experiencing it! Not only is this ideal for your prospect or client, but it's great for your business. Being prepared in advance is what catapults your confidence and helps you be the best coach you can be, which allows you to enjoy your business and be fully present for every moment of your client's journey.

Focusing Forward

Our process of focusing forward is something I do with my team before any project and something we also take our clients through when they begin a program with us.

Focusing forward is a simple (yet outrageously effective) five-step process:

1. Think about what your life and business will look like on the day you reach a particular goal. For example, when your business is successful, what will it look like?

2. Identify what success will mean to you when you've reached that future moment, and how it will positively impact your business, your life, and your entire world. For example, when your business is successful, how will that success positively impact other areas of your life?

3. Look at where you are today and identify the most promising path from here to success.

4. Identify what *might* potentially get in your way and prevent you from being successful in your project.

5. Identify your contingency plan for how to handle each scenario *if* any should arise.

When my team and I do this before a project, we'll often grab a giant flip chart, tear out the pages and write on them, then post them side by side on the wall. Try doing something similar with printer paper or notebook pages to get the same big-picture view on *your* wall or desk!

Take about fifteen minutes to think through the first three steps. Then, for the fourth step of the process, list any potential barriers to success on the left side of a sheet of paper (or the first column in a table if you prefer to make digital notes). This also is your time and space to release all of your doubts and fears about the project without having any solutions in mind; just dump out anything that could possibly prevent you from being your best and giving 100 percent.

Once you've exhausted every possible scenario, then you move on to the fifth step. Go back through each item you listed in the previous step and ask yourself, "*If* this thing were to happen, what could I do to solve the problem?"

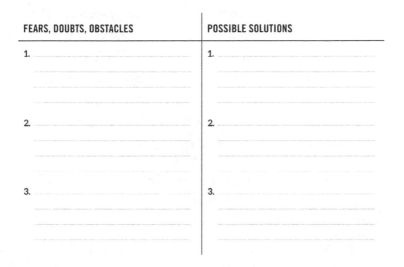

FEARS, DOUBTS, OBSTACLES	POSSIBLE SOLUTIONS
1.	1.
2.	2.
3.	3.

Focusing forward:
Potential obstacles and contingency plans

Write a solution on the right-hand side of the page next to every single one of your concerns and challenges (however ludicrous or unlikely it may be). What the left side of the page represents most often are your fears and doubts, a.k.a. your villains (remember Perfect Portia?). Chances are, when you have support or added momentum from a good program, those villains will never even show their faces. But by focusing forward and considering how you might handle every potential problem, you gain fierce confidence to move forward in reality and increase the likelihood of reaching your goal.

When our students first enroll in a program, we ask them to write a letter to their future self about why they were successful with the program. This exercise lets them get very specific on how they define success. And when they have a clear picture in their minds of what success on their own terms will look and feel like, it dramatically increases their engagement and forward progress!

When we hold on to our fears and villains, then what we spend our energy resisting will manifest in our world. But by expressing them in advance, two things happen:

1. You find that their grip is less constricting when they're out in the open, so you can focus better on the possibilities for your best next step.

2. You give yourself the opportunity to take back your power by identifying potential solutions. People who look ahead with an if-then approach to plan possible solutions are more resilient in the face of adversity, while those who have no plan in place are more likely to quit.

When preparedness meets opportunity, success is inevitable!

Favorite Frames

Take a moment to digest what you've just read. Process what you've taken in so you can make room for even more. Below are some of my favorite frames to recap some of the key points in this chapter.

- A cluttered, disorganized space leads to energy-draining distractions and lower-quality work.

- Managing your time really means managing your boundaries and priorities.

- Use the Four Ds: dump it, duplicate it, delegate it, or do it!

- Focus forward with an if-then approach to plan solutions for possible problems in advance and stay resilient in the face of adversity.

Feel free to add your own favorite frames in the space below!

Chapter 5
INTRODUCTION TO THE COACH APPROACH

Business Reimagined

To create a service based business that is aligned with our values and that we feel proud of, we have to take what I call "the coach approach" to building and running our businesses. (And this applies to *all* service-based business owners, not only to coaches!)

Having grown up as the daughter of a minister, service-based ministry and leading by example were practices I was very familiar with and witnessed my dad doing all the time. I also saw this in my mother; as a teacher, she often modeled for her students what she wanted them to do. (Yep, I'm a preacher's kid *and* a teacher's kid!)

I could see that I, and others, learned by example better than we could learn alone or under pressure from a demanding authority figure. When we see others doing something, we're empowered to learn from them and adopt their methods to suit our own personal style. My experience with this service-based approach, as opposed to a more dominating or dictating style of leading, was that it was also aligned with the essence of coaching.

It felt natural to me to apply the skills of coaching to growing my business. As I leveraged my coaching skills and service-based approach while defining my niche, building my list, facilitating enrollment conversations, presenting my offer, and serving my clients, I reinvented the way I did each of those things by applying the core skills of coaching.

Not only was it fun, but my natural inherent skills as a coach were way more effective (and felt better and more aligned with my own values) than the more traditional approaches to business!

The Coach Approach

The old ways of business are no longer attractive or acceptable to many service-based entrepreneurs. The following list begins to convey the distinction between the coach approach (the "I'd rather" part of the statement) and the traditional way of building and running a business.

- I'd rather embrace collaboration than competition.
- I'd rather support prospective clients in determining their next best step than manipulate them into buying.

- I'd rather leverage referrals than make cold calls.

- I'd rather align my pricing with the value of the transformation than gouge my clients for the highest amount possible.

- I'd rather expand my niche than exclude people who genuinely need my coaching and are ready to commit to the journey.

- I'd rather be curious than believe I already know it all.

- I'd rather leverage technology to cultivate personalized connections than use sterile tech hacks that keep me disconnected from my clients.

- I'd rather seek help along the way than stay isolated while learning through trial and error.

The coach approach doesn't only help you to build and grow your business by applying your coaching skills. It also helps you to do it in a way that's fully aligned with your personality, your passion, and your ideal lifestyle so that you avoid burnout and make every moment count.

Most of the world accepts the old-school way of building a business as the only true way. They believe it should be hard work and no fun, and that you should take pride in being a workaholic. Instead, use the coach approach and leverage your natural gifts and skill sets to feel confident and professional from Day One.

Business Beyond the Masculine

There's a place and a necessity for the masculine approach to business, but it's far past time for the feminine to take her seat at the table as well! The feminine approach to business is a key aspect of the coach approach that I just described to you. But I'm not saying the feminine should drive out the masculine. This is not an either-or scenario; both approaches bring value."

What do I mean by masculine and feminine approaches? Let's start with what I *don't* mean. By masculine and feminine, I'm not referring about prejudicial stereotypes of men and women. I'm talking about internal characteristics that we all possess in varying and variable degrees, whether we identify as a man, a woman, or any other sex or gender identity, and regardless of our gender expression.

The masculine approach is the one that's traditionally been applied in the business world. It's all about systems, processes, campaigns, schedules, targets, efficiency, sales, and profit margins—keeping your nose to the grindstone, working diligently every day to gain an edge. This approach has high success potential, but when taken to an unhealthy extreme, the masculine approach becomes "success at any cost."

The feminine approach is the one that's traditionally been applied in the world of home, family, and friendship. It's all about nurturing, caring, supporting, and creating—paying attention to intuitions, cultivating a healthy and happy lifestyle, and constantly collaborating to reach mutual goals. This may make you a great coach, but at the extreme end of the spectrum, the feminine approach becomes "love at any cost," including sacrificing your business goals.

I have witnessed some women (myself included, many years ago) going to great lengths to avoid expressing or applying their feminine side for fear of being trapped by the traditional stereotype of passive femininity. They fear that people will take femininity for weakness, so to look and feel stronger, they adopt the masculine "success at any cost" attitude. But, as a result, they sway too far toward the extreme masculine and hit resentment and burnout fast because they've ignored their soul and authentic voice. The feminine values of self-care, sustainability, spiritual fulfillment, and social impact provide the courage and inspiration for our masculine values in the day-to-day tasks and activities, as well as the impetus to care for ourselves, our clients, and our quality of life.

Speaking of taking things to extremes, all too often I've seen respected female leaders preach and teach the feminine way of doing business, only to disrespect or dismiss the masculine approach. They want to pull their students away from the masculine into a space of pure femininity. I believe this swing from one extreme end of the spectrum to the opposite extreme is a misguided idea that harms your business and your well-being.

We need both aspects, masculine and feminine, working

in unison for our success to be truly sustainable—not just in business, but also in life. Both play a role in our thoughts, actions, and outcomes: You need masculine business skills to enroll new clients and strategize for your business, and you need feminine skills to serve your clients and facilitate their transformations. The masculine and feminine within you play these parts separately and together, in every aspect of your business.

Think of a river flowing. The water needs the riverbank to provide structure and direction for its progress, and the riverbank needs the water to give it purpose and meaning. So it is in business. The feminine creativity, spirituality, nurturing, and service aspects need the masculine structures of systems, processes, and milestones to experience the freedom of full flow. Our masculine focus on targets and execution needs the feminine fluidity, generosity, and emotional intelligence to innovate, pivot, or collaborate successfully.

With the masculine aspect providing structure, the feminine aspect feels safe and confident to courageously put herself out there to serve. Without structure, it's almost impossible to put yourself out there.

With the masculine aspect implementing automation, the feminine aspect is freed and supported to show up as her best self and offer her best services for the greatest impact. Without automation, your impact can be limited.

The masculine gets strategic and intentional about how to schedule your time, organize your day, and structure yourself and your team, *all in support of* the feminine aim to be your best self living your best life. Without the masculine, the feminine can make great promises but may not be able to deliver on them. Without the feminine, the masculine can burn out and come to regret your passion and life's work. It's the combination of both approaches working together that creates professionalism, credibility, and authenticity for business success with meaningful impact.

It's like a Venn diagram with two intersecting circles. One circle is the masculine side: the strategy, structure, and systems. The second circle is the feminine: the coaching, creativity, and connection.

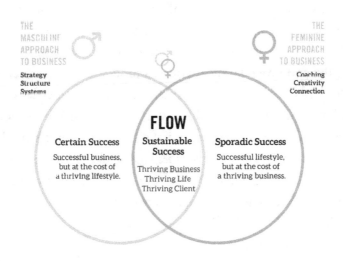

THE MASCULINE APPROACH TO BUSINESS
Strategy
Structure
Systems

THE FEMININE APPROACH TO BUSINESS
Coaching
Creativity
Connection

FLOW

Certain Success
Successful business, but at the cost of a thriving lifestyle.

Sustainable Success
Thriving Business
Thriving Life
Thriving Client

Sporadic Success
Successful lifestyle, but at the cost of a thriving business.

The masculine and feminine in business: Without both aspects, your results start to suffer

At the far end of the masculine circle is burnout, because if you're purely focused on logical, head-down, get-it-done work, then you can't scale, and you can't keep it up for long without a crash. At the far end of the feminine circle is sporadic impact, because if you're purely focused on giving love to your clients, then you risk skipping over the crucial steps that generate consistent results and business success.

Swinging too far into our feminine intentionality of planning and preparing the space for transformation, we might neglect the supporting structures of our businesses. This is how you get stuck in constant prep mode, without ever tipping over into activating all the preparations you've made! On the opposite end of the spectrum, the masculine drive to push for maximum success can spiral into a dark side that has you working on the edge far too often to be healthy and procrastinating from a time-scarcity mindset or to experience the adrenaline rush of a last-minute delivery. To have effective preparations with ample time and without stress, both the masculine and the feminine aspects of the process must *continuously balance and rebalance* each other.

In the space where the two circles of the Venn diagram intersect, that's where you experience *fierce flow* that leads to the freedom of sustainable, scalable growth.

Leveraging Coaching Skills to Build and Run a Better Business

Still with me so far? Great! Let's look at precisely *how* you can apply the coach approach to leverage your existing coaching skills for the benefit of your business.

The core skills of coaching include:

- Listening
- Questioning
- Reflecting
- Empathizing
- Acknowledging
- Strategizing
- Action planning
- Goal setting
- Progress tracking

Take a good look at that list. What do you notice? At the start of the list are feminine skills like listening, reflecting, and empathizing, and in the latter part of the list, you see masculine skills such as strategizing, goal setting, and progress tracking.

To excel in your work as a coach takes both masculine and feminine skills, applied together in an integrated way to facilitate your clients' transformations. And just like it takes these skills to be a great coach, it also takes these exact same skills, both the masculine ones and the feminine ones, to build and run a great coaching business.

To help inspire your thinking, here are a couple examples of how *any* service-based entrepreneur can adopt the coach approach by applying these skills to running their business.

Generating Consistent High-Quality Leads

The coach approach centers on loving and serving people in need of transformation, even if they are not our clients.

When I was growing up, we did a lot of camping. Whether it was just my family or a bigger trip my dad had planned for the youth group, at the end of every trip we'd walk the campsite to pick up any garbage (whether it was ours or not). Mom and Dad always taught us to leave things better than how you found them, so I do the same with my prospects and list building. Whether somebody becomes a client or not, I want to deliver so much value that I've left my prospects better than when I found them.

For example, when you're building your email list, you need to apply the masculine to map out your strategy, funnel structure, targets, milestones, and deadlines, and to navigate the details of implementation. But you also need to apply the feminine to create a service-based strategy, such as providing value through lead magnet content to attract aligned contacts, crafting an effective nurture sequence to build a relationship, and establishing trust by providing value. The feminine approach helps you serve and nurture your prospects until they're ready to take the next step, leaving them better than when you found them.

So, the coach approach to list building takes *both masculine and feminine*; otherwise, you can have the best lead magnet and nurture series known to humankind, but without a well-structured campaign, it won't be noticed. When you bring in both aspects equally, that's when you're balancing and ready to achieve peak results and optimal flow.

Generating Enrollments

The coach approach enrolls only people who genuinely need and want our services.

The key to successful enrollment conversations is that they are a collaborative dialogue between the coach and the prospect. This is very different from the old-school approach you'll see some people fall back on when they talk about making sales: "Sell, sell, sell, no matter what!"

Have you ever seen the movie *Miracle on 34th Street*? In one scene, the department store Santa Claus tells children's parents where to find the perfect toy for their child, even if it means sending them out of the store he works for. That scene resonates with me as a perfect example of the coach approach—helping the person in front of you make *their* best decision to get *their* ideal outcome.

With the coach approach, you'll never have to persuade,

manipulate, or convince someone to sign up for your services. Instead, you'll apply your coaching skills to the enrollment conversation, actively educating and collaborating with your prospect to get clear about what they want and their level of willingness and commitment, then help them understand their choices and make their best next decision. In Chapter 13, I'll go into more detail about how to have effective enrollment conversations using the coach approach.

Favorite Frames

Take a moment to digest what you've just read. Process what you've taken in so you can make room for even more. Below are some of my favorite frames to recap some of the key points in this chapter.

- Your natural inherent skills as a coach are way more effective (and feel better and more aligned with your own values) than the more traditional approaches to business!

- The coach approach to business helps you avoid burnout and create your ideal lifestyle.

- We need both aspects, masculine and feminine, working in unison for our success to be truly sustainable.

Feel free to add your own favorite frames in the space below!

Chapter 6
THE BUSINESS OF COACHING

The Three Things to Master

I often say to my clients that there are three aspects to coaching that they must master:

1. The skills of coaching
2. The marketing of coaching
3. The business of coaching

I believe it's our responsibility to undergo training to become proficient in the *skills* of coaching. True, we are often born with natural potential and talent, but by sharpening those skills, we can use them more wisely, more effectively, and with intention and purpose.

As for the *marketing* of coaching, you can be the greatest coach in the world, but if you can't generate awareness, capture leads, and enroll clients, then you'll have nobody to coach. Likewise, you can be the greatest coach with the best marketing, but if you don't have a streamlined, efficient back end to your business, then your skills will go untapped, and your marketing will not reach your audience because the systems to support your clients and deliver your marketing are insufficient.

The *business* of coaching focuses on the infrastructure, systems, and processes that organize all the details behind the scenes (the masculine side) so you can consistently generate leads, steadily enroll paying clients, and coach as many clients as you want (the feminine side). It's made up of all the elements that have to be in place so you can provide a great experience and support every client to get results.

Your coaching business will struggle if any one of those three aspects is missing. In fact, without all three aspects, you won't even have a coaching business; instead, you'll have a hobby.

To better understand the business of coaching, let's look at what differentiates a hobbyist who dabbles in coaching, or an employee whose job it is to coach, from a business owner who wants to create a livelihood and business out of coaching.

The hobbyist asks, "How do I find my next client to coach?"

The employed coach asks, "How shall I coach the people assigned to me?"

But the business owner asks, "How can I create a *system* that will provide a never-ending stream of clients to coach?"

When I start talking about business *infrastructure, systems,* and *processes,* most coaches get a glazed look on their face. They start feeling nervous they're going to be confined and limited by structure (that's probably why they left their unrewarding job). But structure breeds freedom. A little bit of intentional structure behind the scenes frees up your time.

The structure, like the riverbank analogy from the previous chapter, is what helps you to confidently put yourself out there. While you may not find systems sexy like I do, by learning, implementing, and then mastering the business of coaching, you'll be able to work smarter, not harder. Your business will be a well-oiled machine working on your behalf.

The Range of Acceptability

Your business is not a static entity. It's always growing and evolving. It's important to remember that what got you *here* won't get you *there*.

My friend Annie Hyman Pratt, a leading authority on building successful teams, taught me about her Range of Acceptability concept. When Annie described how the range narrows over time for what's acceptable, I immediately could see how it applied to a coach's business as well. When you first start out in business, things are simple; your first few clients are often people you know, for example. As you evolve, what you once did to find those initial clients no longer works. The Range of Acceptability has narrowed, and you risk being left on the outside. To keep finding new clients, you have to adjust the systems in place and the approaches you take to enroll new clients so you can stay within the acceptable range.

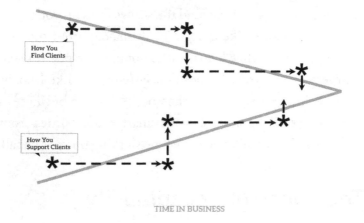

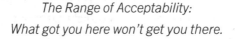

The Range of Acceptability:
What got you here won't get you there.

When the tasks, strategies, and activities you once relied on to generate results start to fall outside the Range of Acceptability, they stop generating results effectively—you hit a plateau or start declining. And the Range of Acceptability changes as our industry and market changes, as our world changes, and also as your own business grows and matures.

As a coach, you just want to coach as many people as you can, making the most impact you can, am I right? But as a business owner, you have to be aware of the evolution of our industry, the shifts in market demand and expectations, and the boundaries of the Range of Acceptability for your business systems. Otherwise, you won't know what success structures are needed to get you to the next level, or where you need to adapt your approach.

To succeed in the business of coaching means knowing how to put the right structures and systems in place so you can leverage your opportunities while feeling confident about what you do. When you set up your business, your offers, and your services in a way that consistently helps clients generate real change, and that evolves over time, you stand out from all the coaches and entrepreneurs who aren't confident enough to facilitate consistent client transformation.

Favorite Frames

Take a moment to digest what you've just read. Process what you've taken in so you can make room for even more. Below are some of my favorite frames to recap some of the key points in this chapter.

- To thrive, you must master the *skills* of coaching, the *marketing* of coaching, and the *business* of coaching.

- Without a streamlined, efficient back end to your business, your skills will go untapped and your marketing will not reach your audience.

- Adjust the systems and approaches of your coaching business to stay inside the Range of Acceptability as it changes over time.

Feel free to add your own favorite frames in the space below!

Chapter 7
THE COACHING
BUSINESS ROADMAP

The Seven Success Structures Every Coaching Business Needs

A few years ago, I created The Coaching Business Roadmap to Success: a one-page infographic that outlines the path every coach must follow to create a confident, efficient, thriving, profitable coaching business that they love, no matter what size they want their business to be.

The roadmap is organized into five phases:

- Phase 0: Foundation
- Phase I: Coaching Client Quick-Start
- Phase II: Optimizing Conversions and Mastering Enrollment
- Phase III: Leveraging
- Phase IV: Scaling

Some coaches don't want to take their business all the way to the higher levels, and that's fine. A coach can have a wildly successful six-figure business just by mastering and optimizing through Phase II.

The seven success structures found throughout the business phases are branding, list building, converting, enrolling, supporting, referring, and leveraging. No matter how big you want your coaching business to grow—whether it's earning $30,000 per year to supplement household income, or like me when I first started and replacing your previous salary of $50,000 per year, or breaking past the six-figure mark—all coaching business owners will travel this path and implement all seven success structures. If you want to work with only a few clients and earn a modest income, then you must still do these things to thrive; you'll just do them in a simpler way and on a smaller scale. If you want to grow larger, you'll optimize these success structures to stay within the Range of Acceptability as you grow.

The Coaching Business Roadmap to Success: Where do you stand today and what's next for your business?

A mistake I hear from new coaches is "Oh, I'm just getting started, Melinda. I don't need all that stuff." And that's precisely why they struggle, experience roller-coaster revenue, or hit plateaus. The structures and systems within their businesses aren't supporting the results they want.

The way in which you maneuver through implementing the roadmap will make *all* the difference between being burdened by your business and being liberated by your business.

First Steps: Introduction to Attracting and Enrolling Clients

To start on the roadmap, let's first look at the initial success structures that focus on generating awareness, building your contact list, and getting clients.

Branding

Did you know that your branding is not about your logo, website, and business cards? You don't need any fancy designs or a specific color palette to be successful! Often, obsessing over these is simply a procrastination tactic designed to keep you in hiding instead of putting yourself out there.

The essence of branding is clear and consistent messaging that resonates with your ideal type of client and aligns with your values. So create messaging that conveys the urgent needs you resolve for your clients. Once you've got that down, you can use it anywhere—in emails, on your website, at networking events, even at dinner parties when someone asks, "So what do you do?"

I learned a simple template from one of my early coaches, Michael Port, from his *Book Yourself Solid* book. When I applied this template into my messaging and conversations, people began to engage and respond.

Your "What I do" message in five easy parts:

1. What type of people do you love to work with? (Keep it simple: just one or two words, max, that describe your ideal clients. For me, it's "coaches.")

2. What are their most urgent needs, stresses, or wants that keep them awake at night? (For my clients, who are coaches, it's "struggling to find clients" and "not making money.")

3. How do you package what you offer? (Again, keep it simple. Just "coaching" is perfect. Other simple examples would be "online course" or "group program.")

4. If they could wave a magic wand, what results do they most want to create? (My clients want to "create a thriving business they feel confident about.")

5. What's the best success story (a client's or your own) you can use to demonstrate that your services have worked for others in similar situations?

Write down your answers to these five questions, then plug your answers into the ready-made template below, and your message is born! You can tweak, refine, perfect, and pivot it at will:

Do you know {answer 1} that are struggling to {answer 2}?

Through my {answer 3}, I help {answer 1} to {answer 4}.

In fact, {answer 5}.

So, do you know any struggling {answer 1}?

Pro tip: One mistake I see people make far too often is that they use wordy, clever phrases that look great written down but take too long (and sound odd) to say out loud in a conversation. So read yours aloud a few times, then edit it until it flows naturally in a conversational style and you can imagine yourself saying it to people without stumbling.

Here's mine as an example:

Do you know <u>coaches</u> that are struggling to <u>find clients and make money</u>?

Through my <u>coaching and software</u>, I help coaches to <u>create a thriving coaching business they feel confident about</u>.

In fact, <u>my client Carol</u> says she used to feel like her business was barely hanging on, as if it were held together by spitballs and duct tape. Now she's running a fulfilling and profitable six-figure coaching business, has plenty of time as a single parent to take care of her two boys, and really gets to feel like she has it all.

So, do you know any struggling <u>coaches</u>?

Practice your message and use your notes initially. Keep practicing until you don't need to check your notes to say the whole thing with confidence. Practice makes permanent.

Another pro tip: Your message will be far more effective if you also do *market research* to validate the words and phrases your ideal type of client actually uses. Market research plays a huge part in branding!

Interview people in your niche, or past clients, for example, using questions two and four from the previous list. Then use the words and phrases they share with you to establish your brand with clarity, using your ideal clients' own language to express your message.

Most coaching schools and mentors don't just guide coaches down the wrong track by focusing too much on the visual aspect of their brand; they also teach that branding requires narrowing down your niche. While it's true that the more focused you can be, the better and faster you'll attract your ideal clients, the methods these schools and mentors are teaching just don't work for most coaches!

They're overly focused on demographics and characteristics of a type of person instead of on people's challenges and results. Your niche is not "women in their fifties" or "parents of teenagers." It's not about demographics or a specific type of person at all! In fact, if you focus on defining your niche by a characteristic like career or age, you'll create an artificial boundary that unnecessarily restricts the number and type of clients you can help. (If you feel boxed in by your niche instead of supported by it, then something is wrong. Your niche should expand in a focused, intentional way, not exclude.)

So don't think of any specific type or group of people right now. Instead, think about the challenges you're best equipped to help people with, and the transformations those people are seeking.

Your niche is composed of the *challenges* your ideal clients face and the *results* they want. For example, when I launched The Coaches Console, it was a solution to the challenge and overwhelm coaches experienced in their businesses. The result was to make their business processes easier so they could confidently get clients, make money, and make an impact. So the emphasis in our marketing has been on the challenges and results. Because my passion is coaching, "coaches" is a clarifier in our marketing. But our emphasis is on the challenges of business and desired outcomes. As a result, we attract all sorts of service-based entrepreneurs (nutritionists, consultants, and therapists, to name a few) that struggle with business. Our niche expands as needed; it doesn't exclude.

List Building

As you move into Phase II of your coaching business, list building takes on a more automated approach. It's time to set up systems that attract the right people so that you can consistently build your list of high-quality leads and prospects. So that list building doesn't take over your entire life, you need to *automate* the process, while still maintaining a personal connection with your prospects and clients.

Your list of contacts is your number one asset. To attract your ideal clients to your list, you first have to be of service. That's how the right people will come to know, like, and trust you, and that's what prompts them to hire you, rehire you, and refer you. And that's why it's a good idea to offer a lead magnet, a free yet valuable resource that you give away in exchange for contact information.

Your lead magnet should not simply offer information, because information can be found everywhere (remember we're beyond the Information Age)! What people really want and value is the *right* information to help them see results fast and build their momentum in an area in which it has been tough for them to make progress. Share with them *what* they need to know and *why* it's important for them to know it (but never the *how*—that's where your packages and programs come in). By being of service to them in this way, you create engagement and the beginnings of a relationship.

Here's a simple lead magnet outline for your coaching business:

1. The cover page: a concise, result-based title for your lead magnet.

2. Some content that conveys the niche this resource is designed to serve and describes the challenges your ideal clients face, painting a picture of possibility for them to overcome their struggles and achieve their dreams.

3. A welcome to your readers, validating their thoughts and feelings, and reminding them that they picked up your free resource for a reason.

4. Reassurance that they are not alone—that you've met and helped others like them overcome the same challenges to thriving success, and that similar success is achievable for them too.

5. A high-level overview of the steps in the journey of transformation that takes your clients from overwhelm to results.

6. Coaching exercises to help your prospect complete action items and accomplish milestones for the first step in the journey of transformation.

7. A tip to help maintain momentum or a pitfall they should avoid as they start the journey.

8. A call to action to book a sample session with you, rather than continuing to face their challenges alone.

9. A short blurb about you, the coach.

To accompany your lead magnet, you'll also need these items:

• An opt-in page and opt-in form where people can learn about your resource and enter their email address to receive a copy of your lead magnet.

• A thank-you page that people see only after they opt in for your lead magnet.

• A series of automated emails sent out to your new

subscribers to follow up with them and nurture the relationship.

- A way to segment your contacts list so that you can send the right message to the right people for optimal conversions.

- A way to measure and track the results of the list-building funnel you've built, so you can see how well it's working.

When you have all of these items working together, and the whole list-building funnel is automated, you can literally wake up in the morning and see how many people have added themselves to your list overnight.

Converting

To go from a list of prospects to new paying clients, you need a conversion strategy. (And that strategy should not be exclusively hope-based!)

The key step in the conversion process is to have a sample session with your prospect. This could be a session that you charge a fee for, or it could be a free session. People use a bunch of different names for it, but its purpose is for you and your prospect to have an enrollment conversation.

Note: A sample session is *not* just a coaching session where you hope their excitement is so great that they'll ask you to work with them. A sample session is more than that. It's an intentionally designed conversation, with coaching woven through it to help them experience what it's like working with you (more about this conversation in Chapter 13).

And one of the ways to get people to book a session with you is to create a result-based name for the session itself. By now, you've done some market research and identified the biggest, most urgent challenges your ideal clients face and the transformation they're looking for. So we need to use that information to generate a name based on the results you offer—a name that conveys the value in your ideal clients' language.

So here's how to do that:

1. List the top three results your ideal clients want (in their words). This is List A.

2. List several terms that describe the type of session in generic terms (*consultation, discovery session, exploratory session*, etc.) This is List B.

3. Read out one description from List A, followed by one term from List B. (Here are a few examples of what this might look like: Revive Your Relationship Discovery Session, Create a Career You Love Consultation, Maximum-Impact Business Strategy Session.)

4. Now pick one title. Share it with your audience or previous clients. How do they respond? Research

the feedback you get. If it resonates with others, keep using it. If it doesn't, choose another one from the list.

So long as you have a good understanding of the results your ideal clients want, you'll always be able to craft a compelling session title that maximizes your chances of converting prospects to enrollment conversation appointments.

Enrolling

What we as coaches call "enrolling," most people call "sales."

You know why I don't call it "sales"? Because as the coach in an enrollment conversation, our job is *not* to "make sales"—it's to enroll, support, and guide people to their best next step that will change their lives! In most cases, it will lead to them hiring you.

The old-school, sales-oriented approach can be persuasive, but in a pushy, imposing way. It's designed to defend against objections rather than resolve them, and to make the sales goal at any cost. This approach creates tension between the salesperson and the prospect, because they're coming to the conversation with very different goals. The prospect wants to navigate their way to a crucial transformation, while the salesperson just wants to sell, sell, sell.

Contrast this with the coach approach to enrollment. The coach approach is compelling because it's designed to acknowledge objections and explore the root issues underlying them so they can be resolved or reframed. This approach creates a partnership between the coach and the prospect, because they're working together toward the same goal: the next best step for the potential client. The prospect wants to navigate their way to a crucial transformation, and the coach wants to support and facilitate that transformative journey.

When you "sell" from a place of service, it doesn't feel like selling! It's more of an invitation. That's the beauty of the coach approach.

To make this easier for you to plan and implement, I'll go into a lot more detail about attracting and enrolling your ideal clients in Chapter 13, including my own ten-part enrollment conversation outline. Plus, I'll give you the full lowdown on the four most common objections and how to overcome them.

For now, let's focus on an important aspect that affects your success in enrollment conversations: the way in which you convey your packages and pricing options.

For the longest time, coaches followed the model of other service businesses in using a time-based approach to packages and pricing. So throughout the Information Age, we got used to charging per session or per month. But the problem with this approach is that when your rate is time-based, your buyer becomes focused on only the two dimensions you're showing them: time and money. So they naturally want to get the most time for the lowest price, because that's the measure of value in this pricing model.

Instead of basing your packages and pricing on time, what if you based them on results? With this approach, the focus immediately points to the results your buyer can achieve with your support. Your prospect can see the value in your services and is no longer trying to get the best deal on your time. And you're able to include more than just the coaching sessions as part of their package, because it isn't priced by the time you spend in sessions. For example, your package could include accountability tools, online coaching between sessions, and other resources to support your client in getting results.

Applying the coach approach and basing your offer on results rather than time means that your coaching feels even more valuable, you get to support your clients in even more ways, and they get the results that matter most to them.

Favorite Frames

Take a moment to digest what you've just read. Process what you've taken in so you can make room for even more. Below are some of my favorite frames to recap some of the key points in this chapter.

- The way you move through the roadmap to coaching business success makes all the difference between being burdened by your business or liberated by it.

- Your branding is not about your logo, your website, or your business cards.

- Your niche is composed of the challenges your ideal clients face and the results they want.

- When you "sell" from a place of service, it doesn't feel like selling!

- Explore result-based pricing to benefit your clients and your business.

Feel free to add your own favorite frames in the space below!

Chapter 8
MOVING FARTHER
ALONG THE ROADMAP

Next Steps:
From Supporting to Leveraging

As we move farther along the roadmap, let's look at the remaining success structures every coaching business needs.

Supporting

After you've found your newest clients and they've invested in your coaching package or program, what next? There's a gap of time between them saying yes and the moment of either their first session or getting started in your program.

But if you pay no attention to what happens in that gap, then all the momentum and courage your new client felt in that *yes* moment of enrollment will stall before they ever get started, and that's how buyer's remorse kicks in. It's not enough to make the sale and then deliver the service. We need to roll out the red carpet, onboard our new clients into our business, and create a great experience by supporting them right out of the gate. It's important to help them build momentum with a few quick wins; otherwise, they'll get overwhelmed on Day One!

To onboard new clients, address the obstacles that will prevent them from getting started, or equip them with what they need to start off with a bang. This can be done through sending automated email messages, or providing simple pre-work exercises or a list of materials to gather before they get started. Your onboarding series of emails should do the following for your new clients:

- Acknowledge and validate the courage it took for them to commit to their transformation.

- Connect the dots explicitly between what they're going to do and the results they're going to get. (Remind them why it's important to them so they continue to prioritize the work that lies ahead!)

- Prompt and encourage them to engage with your community and share their successes, ideas, or questions.

- Focus forward on their future and the qualities needed for success. (The more they cultivate those qualities, in advance, the easier it gets to keep going should challenges arise.)

- Celebrate the successes of others as examples of what's possible. (Identify the points in the journey of transformation where your clients most often get stuck, and share stories of people who've overcome those particular situations to give your clients hope and faith.)

- Provide prep work that, when completed, will equip them to be an even better client.

When preparedness meets great content and a great experience, then transformative results are inevitable. This is also why your support should not falter or diminish as your client progresses further into the coaching relationship. I teach my clients to deliver what I call "Exquisite Client Support" that goes beyond the coaching session.

As coaches, we have the responsibility to put whatever resources we can behind supporting our clients to get results. This level of passion for providing support is what turns your clients into raving fans who rehire you, refer you, and may even become strategic referral partners with you. So how do you implement Exquisite Client Support? Here are just a few examples of the essentials that I recommend for our clients.

Support *before* the session:

- Your client receives a branded, time zone–specific automated appointment reminder with the necessary details to make it easy to prepare and connect.

- Your client completes the Call Strategy Form included in the automated appointment reminder and submits it back to you twenty-four hours prior to the coaching session.

- You review the answers submitted on the Call Strategy Form before each session and prepare yourself to address those things in the session.

Support *during* the session:

- You record the session, with your client's permission, so your client doesn't have to scribble notes the whole time (and you don't have to remember what you said when you were in the zone).

- You store your private notes, thoughts, and observations from the session in a secure, confidential client portal so that you can use these to inform the support you provide for the client in the future (and easily put your hands on everything when you need it).

Support *after* the session:

- Your automated system sends a Post-Session Recap Form to every client after every appointment.

- The client answers the simple questions on this form in your secured, confidential client portal to turn their aha moments from the session into actionable steps and new habits.

- You post the video or audio recording in your secure, client portal for your client to replay on demand.

Support *between* sessions:

- You give your clients access to a private portal where they can post questions, share celebrations, and upload homework or documents to be reviewed.

- Your client commits to using this private portal at any time if they feel stuck in between each session.

- When your client indicates they need support between sessions, you send them a quick response with immediate advice as well as a plan to address the issue in more depth at your next session if needed. This provides just-in-time online coaching to help your client maintain momentum and progress.

With all of this support, your clients are fully empowered to make the most of their coaching package or your program.

Referring

No matter what phase of maturity your business is in, referrals are an excellent way to leverage other people's lists to help build your own and to get new clients and maintain or grow your coaching income.

By *referrals*, I don't mean vague recommendations, like when someone tells you that you should watch a certain movie or try a recipe they enjoy! Anybody can do that; it's a simple, low-cost, low-risk suggestion, which is very different from the high value of your coaching services. And I don't mean someone casually passing your website URL or email address on to an interested friend with a quick "Tell them I sent you," either. That's not a true referral; it's a cold, unqualified lead.

A real referral is different. A good, qualified referral is "done business." It means that your referral partner, knowing everything they know about your business and the type of ideal client you're looking for, has decided that your services are a good fit for someone in their circles. The referral partner has done the legwork to vet both parties before making the introduction.

A good referral is when:

- You've spoken with the referral partner and they're clear about your offer and your ideal client.

- You've shared your client success stories, content assets, and other pre-written resources so it's easy for the referral partner to make referrals and introductions.

- They've identified one or multiple people among their contacts who are a good fit.

- They're happy to introduce you to those people, or to speak to them and let them know why they're referring you.

- You're happy to reciprocate, not necessarily by promoting your referral partner or referring people to their business, but by doing whatever is the most appropriate thing you can do to help your referral partner reach a goal or overcome a challenge.

But referrals don't "just happen" unless you pave the way by preparing your business in advance to succeed. So many business owners leave referrals to chance, thinking, "People know I'm good at what I do. If they know someone who's a good fit, they'll send them my way." Nope! Even for your most loyal supporters with the best of intentions, sending you referrals is not top of mind. But when you set up a streamlined referral request process and automate it, you make prompting those referrals effortless for your partners *and* effortless for you.

The following prompts will help you implement an intentional referral process:

- Provide an online booking tool that makes it easy for prospects referred to you to book a convenient time and date to talk with you so there's no confusion about time zones or who's calling whom.

- Send your prospects automated appointment reminders, along with a form they can fill out for the sample session.

- Implement a *No, not yet* nurture sequence to follow up with prospects who aren't ready to become clients just yet.

To help you stand out from others when someone passes you a referral, what matters is sharing your experience with the prospect and being clear about the results they can expect. I like to wow my prospects before they even become clients. This starts with reducing your prospect's overwhelm, never adding to it! When prospects experience a high level of professionalism from you, they feel confident that you have the skill set and business acumen to support them.

- Keep a record of which referral partner introduced you to whom.

- Track which referrals became clients, and which offer(s) they bought.

When a referral partner leverages their trust with their audience and passes referrals to you, it's very helpful for them to know if the referral was successful or not. If you let them know if a referral became a client, then they're in a better position to send you more or better referrals the next time! But if they have no idea if their referrals became clients, that often leads to them not sending any more your way.

- Schedule time to reach out to referral partners after they pass you a new referral, and automate this follow-up process.

Following up with referral partners to say thanks or to debrief how the referral process went will go a long way to continue to strengthen your relationship, encouraging further referrals.

- Create a process to prompt and collect referrals from every client. I have created an email that is automatically sent to every client thirty days before their client agreement ends that asks them who they might know and to share referral information.

Your current clients can often be your greatest source of referrals—if you're intentional about it. They're in the midst of creating change and receiving benefit from working with you. They're becoming your raving fans. Automating the process for existing clients makes it easy for them to quickly think of people who could benefit in similar ways. Once you've implemented these seven tasks, you'll be ready for more and better referrals than you ever expected.

Leveraging

This success structure really comes into play as you make the move along the roadmap from Phase III into Phase IV and beyond. This is where you leverage your time and resources to reach more people. At the core of your business is your one-on-one coaching. But working one-on-one allows you to help only a limited number of people.

By this phase of your business, you've worked with enough clients to notice that you're sharing common resources with every client, asking the same coaching questions, and basically repeating yourself to each client because they share similar challenges and patterns. When you collect all of those resources, common questions, and redundant tips and put them together, you have the core content for an offer that could serve multiple clients at the same time!

When you use online content or group programs to support your clients, you can help far more people simultaneously, without lots of extra time or effort on your part—like when we enrolled three hundred people into our Coaching Business System program or had over fourteen hundred people register for our Business of Coaching LIVE three-day training event. In fact, by leveraging your resources, you can spend less time working with more people. It can be a smarter way to work. Let's look at the following example to demonstrate this point of leverage:

Business A has twenty private, one-on-one clients. Those clients take up twenty hours each week. There's still plenty of time for marketing and other business activities.

Business B has five private clients and one group program of twenty clients. This coach is now working with five additional clients while taking up a total of only six hours each week.

Whether you create an online course, set up a group coaching program, offer a membership community, or host a live virtual event, you can create a bigger ripple effect in the world. To figure out how online courses or programs fit into your practice and your business, think about the journey of transformation that your clients take to get their desired outcomes. Ask yourself what the *minimum* you could include in your offer to help a group would be so they get the promised results. And also ask what the *biggest, most comprehensive* thing you could offer to help them make progress on that journey to reach their destination would be.

Maybe you offer a group coaching program or an online course as an intermediate step, a smaller commitment that people can make before they're ready to enroll in your one-on-one signature coaching package. Maybe you set up an online course with integrated coaching that takes many clients through the same process they'd experience in your private coaching. Maybe you create a premium back-end program that becomes the natural next step for your clients after a period of one-on-one coaching.

When you find your leverage to multiply your impact (without multiplying your workload), your coaching business can become the scalable, transformation-generating machine you always knew it could be!

Favorite Frames

Take a moment to digest what you've just read. Process what you've taken in so you can make room for even more. Below are some of my favorite frames to recap some of the key points in this chapter.

- Help new clients build momentum with a few quick wins so they don't feel overwhelmed.

- Implement Exquisite Client Support before, during, after, and in between every coaching session.

- Referrals don't just happen, unless you pave the way by preparing your business in advance.

- When you gather together all the advice, answers, and resources you most often share with clients, you already have the core content for a group program.

Feel free to add your own favorite frames in the space below!

Chapter 9
TECHNOLOGY AND YOUR COACHING BUSINESS

The Tech You Need
(Everything Else, You Can Ignore)

Almost every coach I've coached with worries about getting more clients—because that's how coaching works, right? The more clients you help, the more fulfilling and profitable your business becomes?

Not quite. Of course, your practice needs paying clients, but the truth is that without the right systems in place, you could spend *years* struggling and still never fill your books.

So don't ask yourself, "How do I get more clients?" Instead, ask a different question: "How do I prepare my business and create systems to consistently deliver results?"

Once you set up the right success structures to ensure reliable results for your clients, you'll find that getting clients (and profits) are almost effortless, and they keep on coming.

After that, growing your practice even further is only a matter of scale based on your goals.

To get these success structures set up, you're going to need the right technology. Now, this is the point where some of the clients I work with try to hide their head under a blanket and abdicate all responsibility for a variety of reasons:

- "But I'm no good with technology!"
- "But I've never used that tool before!"
- "I can't even make sense of {insert your most hated and bewildering technology here}!"
- "I've never been one to automate funnels and communications. That takes away the personalization for each client!"
- "What if I do it wrong?"
- "What if it's too damn hard?"

The blankie is a big giveaway that this is fear-based, reactive thinking! And that same thinking will keep you and your business curled up small instead of growing into your true power and potential.

Trust me on this: Not only do you have all the skills and capability you need to figure this tech stuff out, but you also don't need as much as you probably think. And it doesn't have to be hard to piece together, because you can use a software platform that combines and controls multiple useful tools in one place. This is why we developed The Coaches Console to be the most full-featured, fully integrated platform designed specifically for coaching businesses!

Let's start by pinpointing the level of business maturity you're at with your coaching business. If you don't know the level you're at, you may start reaching for tools you don't really need yet, or you might be missing a vital tool that could streamline your path to swift success.

At the earliest stage of maturity, your coaching business is not yet a business. It's an idea, a plan, a hobby, or an obsession even, but you haven't taken it beyond that. You realize you have a talent for helping people, and you love the buzz you get from it, but you aren't trying to make coaching profitable yet. If you're in this phase right now, you don't currently have any specific technology needs, but now's the time to list what you're going to need next and get those systems prepared in advance. (The way my friend and colleague Michelle Schubnel of Group Coaching Success puts it is to set things up for the business you want, not the business you have. So focus forward and plan for your future success.)

When you stop dabbling and start to build your business in all seriousness, you'll move through the next four phases of business maturity one by one. Each phase can last anywhere from a few months to years, depending on how quickly and how solidly you set up success structures to support your growth. And yep, these five phases (from hobbyist to Phase IV) are the same phases from the roadmap I showed you earlier.

In Phase I, you've moved beyond coaching as a hobby and started looking for paying clients, but you don't have enough leads and prospects on your list to ensure you can keep the business going and pay yourself consistently. You might find sporadic clients from the people you already know. Your fees are time-based, your income is sporadic, and you're probably making less than $30,000 per year.

In Phase II, you're committed to building a coaching business that generates steady, reliable income for you and great results for your clients. You're consistently making up to $50,000 per year, maybe more, but you've hit a plateau and feel you're not booking enough enrollment conversations or enrolling enough new clients to grow your business any further.

In Phase III, you've experienced the ripple effect your work has on the world, and you're inspired! Your revenue is approaching or has just surpassed six figures and you're ready to keep on growing, but you feel like there's never enough time to do everything you'd like to get done. You want to leverage your time in new ways and expand the offerings in your business for optimal growth and impact.

In Phase IV, your coaching business has evolved into a mission and a movement that will change the lives of thousands, maybe even millions. To execute your vision in greater and greater ways, you're expanding your team. Your revenue is consistently in the six-figure range and possibly well on the way to seven figures, and you're confident in your next move.

Now take a look at what technology you *really* need if you're in Phase I...and what else you need to add for the later phases of maturity:

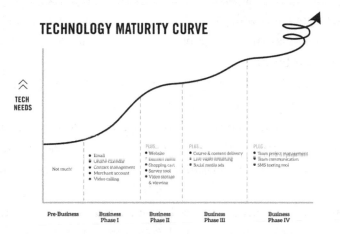

The tech you need: Your tool set will change as your business grows; choose tools that grow with you!

In the first phase, most of the tools aren't new to you, such as email and an online calendar. Honestly, if you don't already have those two (and use them pretty regularly), I'd be surprised!

But to have a secure version of each of these technologies that you can use with your prospects and clients while protecting their data and confidentiality to a professional standard, you might want to consider getting a fully secured online communication platform that handles both. And you may as well have your merchant account for easy payment processing integrated into the same platform, making another potentially complex tool simple to use.

As your coaching business matures, you'll need to expand your technology tool set—and the tools you use must not only play nicely together but also be able to scale alongside your business.

You'll add a website and shopping cart before you shift into selling your coaching offers online in Phase II, you'll add a course and content delivery system before you branch out into offering online courses or community memberships in Phase III, and so on. Obviously, it helps if your new course and content delivery system will "talk" to your existing online calendar, shopping cart, and contact management system! Keeping as much of your technology as possible within one integrated platform as you grow is the simplest way to avoid overwhelm and control all of your business success structures with minimal investment of your time and energy.

The best way to get this right is to work backward. So first determine your business goals. What size do you think you want your coaching business to grow to? What level of revenue do you think you'll need to sustain your business at that size? Then you can reverse engineer your list of technology requirements based on your goals so that you can look to integrate as many of those technologies as possible in one platform.

The fewer technology platforms you use to manage your business, and the more processes you can integrate into a single technology platform, the easier it is to launch and grow your business. When entrepreneurs hit a plateau, it's rarely a sales or marketing issue holding them back. Much more often, it's about systems issues because your technology is not supporting and integrating efficient systems. (In other words, your tech is no longer within the Range of Acceptability.)

Your level of overwhelm is often directly related to the number of tech tools and apps you have to patch together. Having an integrated technology plan keeps things streamlined and simple so that your back office runs efficiently without *you* having to do everything. It's the magic behind the scenes that transforms your business back end from a burden to a blessing.

The Power of an Integrated Back Office

Implementing the seven success structures from the previous chapters will go a long way to making your business successful while reducing your overwhelm. But implementing each one is not all there is to it! It's how these individual systems and the different technology platforms you use are connected and integrated, working together, that simplifies your coaching business and makes it easier and quicker to get sustainable, scalable results.

If you've always felt like you must be missing something in your coaching business, a lack of integrated systems is probably the reason why. You need systems *and* integration to make your business work for you so you don't have to work so hard for your business.

Without integration, setting up the things your business needs, like effective marketing, sales, and client support, gets so complex that it feels overwhelming, and the attempts you do make are disjointed. One of my clients told me when I first met her "my business was being held together with spitballs and duct tape," while another said her "business back end felt like a big pile of spaghetti." No wonder so many coaches aren't consistently getting great results in their business or for their clients. No wonder so many coaches are hitting plateaus and can't grow past them. Their own back office stacks the odds against them, because an unstructured, patchwork tech approach just can't sustain a thriving coaching practice that generates real transformation!

The integrated technology infrastructure of your business is what frees you to deliver the transformation you promise and leverage your time. Integration means all of the technology is "talking" to each other and working together without you having to manage it all, just like a series of gears interlocks and one helps the other operate effectively. With integration, you're moving smoothly forward. Without it, you're reinventing the wheel and stuck in reactive mode, always scrambling to catch up.

But integration doesn't happen by magic. *What* you integrate matters just as much as *how* you integrate it. You need your back-office infrastructure to integrate all the best practices of a thriving coaching practice so that it becomes a well-oiled machine.

That means you need to get at least the essentials in place *before* you start trying to fill your schedule with new client appointments. Otherwise, each time you get new clients, the "oh crap, now what" scramble just continues.

It's crucial to know up front the existing best practices for your coaching business that you just learned from the Coaching Business Roadmap *and* how they work together. Too often, we learn them in segmented, isolated ways, taking one class on marketing, then later another class on sales, or a different training on list building. But often we don't step back and see how it all fits together, and how one thing should transition seamlessly into the next!

This disconnected, disjointed experience of your business's back end is what leaves you spending more time and working harder on it than you should. It's important to know the best practices, of course, but it's much more important to understand how they integrate and function together.

Favorite Frames

Take a moment to digest what you've just read. Process what you've taken in so you can make room for even more. Below are some of my favorite frames to recap some of the key points in this chapter.

- Keep asking, "How do I prepare my business and create systems to consistently deliver results?"

- Your technology needs are determined by your business's maturity and your desire to step up to the next phase.

- Integrated technology creates scalable, sustainable results without extra time or effort from you.

- What you integrate matters just as much as how you integrate it.

Feel free to add your own favorite frames in the space below!

Chapter 10
MARKETING THAT FITS YOUR BUSINESS

Eight Ways to Get Your First (or Next) Client

In Chapters 7 and 8, I stated that to get clients, you first need to set up the success systems to enroll them, onboard them, support them, and ensure they get results. And I've shown you the tech tools you'll need at each stage as your business matures.

But I haven't forgotten the pressing need to ensure that your coaching business has enough clients to *stay* in business! So now, let's look at the eight core marketing tactics that I'm seeing work for coaches in today's world.

Getting Clients in Coaching Business Phase I

In Phase I, you don't have a lot of resources or a team behind you, so you need to start with a tactic that's easy, cost-effective, and quick to set up. I recommend any of these four:

Networking. Whether it's your personal network or you're engaging with strategic referral partners, what matters is that you educate your contacts on how to *spot* an ideal referral for you and how to *make* that referral. That means you need to help them understand the essence of the results your coaching business offers and the type of client that's the best fit. (We'll look at networking in more detail in Chapter 11.)

Writing. If you enjoy writing, then leverage that talent and passion into sharing articles for others to distribute or post, or by being a guest blogger. The idea is to identify people who are serving your ideal clients, but in different ways and with different services from your own; then you leverage their list to grow yours. So if you're a business coach, you might reach out to website designers, for example, or if you're a life coach, you could reach out to holistic therapists or spiritual teachers. Invite them to share your article—which includes a call to action for people to give you their email address—with their audiences.

Giving interviews. If speaking comes naturally to you, then leveraging other people's podcasts can be a quick, easy way to get in front of your ideal audience. Podcast owners are always looking for guests to interview. The idea, again, is to identify those people who are serving the same audience as you, but in different ways, and then engage their audience by providing value through content in your interview, and sharing a free resource the listeners can access when they give you their name and email address.

Offering free coaching. I'm not talking about offering short sample sessions that are poorly disguised sales calls, or even taking on endless pro bono clients because you're unsure of yourself, but an actual coaching call in which you do real work, intentionally free of charge. Sure, it costs you time, but if you don't have enough paying clients yet, then you can afford to spend some of the time you *would* be working with clients to make sure you *get* clients to work with. Nothing demonstrates the power of great coaching like...great coaching! Some of your best prospects who weren't quite ready to buy will decide they're ready once they've experienced your coaching for themselves and you invite them to become your client. (If you choose this tactic, I'll share a tip: Use it sparingly or you could fall into the trap of having all pro bono clients. And let your free coaching clients know that, if they are happy with their experience, in exchange you would like them to provide a client testimonial that you can share in your marketing materials or on your website.)

These four marketing tactics are the easiest; cost the least in terms of money, effort, and time; and help you "get yourself out there" fast so you can see results sooner. Many newer coaches in Phase I don't yet have the clarity to create all the necessary content or put together what they need for other marketing tactics, so trying to do anything more complicated will only slow you down in getting your first clients on the books.

Getting Clients in Coaching Business Phase II

In Phase II you're getting some traction under your belt: You're learning and implementing the foundations for list building, doing market research, understanding enrollments better, learning how to talk and engage with your audiences. And all of that means it's now easier for you to create effective content. So let's start leveraging that ability with these next four marketing tactics!

> **Speaking.** This could mean talking on a small live stage at an event for local associations and organizations; it could mean a bigger talk at an international conference; it could be a webinar, workshop, podcasts or any other live event (in person or virtual). The key is that you speak on topics of interest to your ideal clients, gain an opportunity to build relationships with the audience members, and have a system set up to capture the contact

details of those who are the best fit for your offer (or the best fit to become a new strategic referral partner). It could be from your own stage or you could be a guest speaker on someone else's stage. A good speaking gig can bring a slew of new, qualified leads onto your list, or generate sales directly, when you do it right!

Creating online challenges. These have really picked up speed in recent years in the coaching industry. They're often run on a social network, but I've seen some coaches get results with challenges delivered via email or blog posts too. The idea is to create a fun, engaging "challenge" that typically lasts three to seven days, with short and simple daily activities for participants to complete. These activities are designed to help people to make quick, small wins in a situation that's been challenging for them. The value they experience through quick wins and immediate momentum will deepen the know-like-trust factor by *experiencing* that your advice gets results. People hire you when they know you, like you, and trust you. Those that get results and want more will be primed and ready to be your next paying clients.

Email marketing. Whether you're sending a short, simple email series to people in your list of contacts or going for a full-on launch campaign to promote your newest offer, this tactic requires you to have some people on your email list—whether it's just fifty or five hundred. (That's why I like starting with networking in Phase I, as you can leverage other people's lists to help you build your own.) A "seed launch," or "founder's launch," as some call it, can be a quick way to launch a new program or service when you don't have many folks on your list. Once you have an email list, no matter its size, that's an asset your business needs to make the most of! Sending a simple sequence of just three or four emails can gain a lot of traction when you explain your offer, share valuable content, invite your email readers to book a sample session with you, or extend a savings, special deal, or opportunity when someone decides to join as one of your initial "founding clients."

Using social media. You probably already use some social media in your personal life, and maybe you've set up a page or profile for your coaching business on one or two social networks. But leveraging social media strategically to fulfill your intentions for your business takes planning and a systematic set up so that it achieves your goal without taking up too much of your time and energy. To find new clients, focus on the platform your ideal clients use the most and share your most valuable free content with them as well as invite them to share their thoughts and questions with you. You can leverage social media to build your audience (those who like you and follow you), which you can then turn into leads when you invite them to opt in and join your official contact list.

Getting Clients in Coaching Business Phase III or IV

If you're already in Phase III, you can go ahead with any (or a combination) of the eight tactics just described, but at an even higher level, which means sending more complex email campaigns, speaking at bigger events, increasing your findability on search engines and your return on investment in social media ads, and so on. At this point you've already done a lot of work to optimize your content and conversions, so you can layer other tactics—such as offering online launches and live events and inviting multiple referral partners to promote your offer simultaneously—on top of that.

As you enter Phase III, typically your revenue is at a point where you have more revenue to invest into developing and implementing these tactics and hiring experts to optimize that work. That's when you'll know you're moving into Phase IV!

Choosing the Right Marketing Strategy for You

Don't pick a marketing tactic just because you feel like you should, or because some "guru" recommended it and told you it worked for them. Choose the one or two that genuinely appeal to you and naturally align with your personal style and preferences.

Do you love connecting people with the right resources and solutions? Does speaking to a group come naturally?

Does writing light you up? Are you a natural on social media? Choose the marketing tactic that resonates the most with your natural style and give it your fierce focus over several months for consistent results.

Keeping your marketing strategy simple with just one tactic to focus on is often more effective than a complex strategy. So many newer coaches diffuse their energy by trying multiple tactics at the same time, never focusing on just one. Or they try one for a short time, but when they don't experience immediate gratification they just give up and move on to trying something else for a week or two, and so on. That short-term, sporadic approach leads only to sporadic results; it won't work in the long term! Any marketing tactic takes time and consistency to build traction.

I also see coaches in the earlier phases attempting marketing tactics that take quite a bit of time or require a lot of complex technologies to set up and implement. If you start using a tactic before you're ready for it, you won't get the best results—that's why I've organized these eight tactics into those most suitable for Phase I, Phase II, and beyond. It's much more effective (in terms of your time and money) to get clear on your offer and message, gain traction and momentum, and get paying clients *before* you layer in any complexity. Keep it simple to get results.

Depending on which business phase you're in right now—not where you want to be, but where you are *today*—pick just one or two marketing tactics that most resonate with you and put your full focus on that activity for the next ninety days. Set an ambitious yet achievable target for yourself, like, "I will get nine new clients in the next ninety days." Then mark your calendar with that goal to remind you to check in and see how far your new marketing activity has brought you!

Favorite Frames

Take a moment to digest what you've just read. Process what you've taken in so you can make room for even more. Below are some of my favorite frames to recap some of the key points in this chapter.

- Start with the marketing tactics that are easiest; cost the least money, effort, and time; and help you "get yourself out there" fast so you can see results sooner.

- Choose one or two marketing tactics that genuinely appeal to you and naturally align with your personal style and preferences.

- As your business grows and matures, you'll develop the capacity to create highly effective marketing content and increasingly advanced promotional campaigns.

Feel free to add your own favorite frames in the space below!

Chapter 11
THE POWER OF NETWORKING

A Fast, Simple Way to Get Clients

One of the fastest, easiest, *funnest* ways to get new prospects, especially when you're just getting started, is by networking!

"But, Melinda, I hate networking!"

I hear this from a lot of our clients. But when I look at their approach to networking, it's more like socializing followed by hoping someone hires them. If that's your approach to networking, then yeah, I'd probably hate it too! The networking I'm talking about is more intentional and service-based.

What I have found for service-based businesses, especially if you have little time, little experience, or little cash to invest in your marketing, is that *leveraging the trust of strategic referral partners* produces the biggest result with the least effort and requires very little technology.

To make networking pay off for you, all you need are

the mindset, the meeting, and the magic, but you need to avoid mistakes newbie networkers often make.

Even as an introvert, I love networking because you're growing your list and getting clients through building intentional relationships and cultivating trust with strategic referral partners, which is totally in line with the coach approach to business.

The Referral-Oriented Mindset

When you're networking, don't set out to sell your services to the members of the group. While some of the members of your networking group can benefit from your services, many of the people you meet while networking are not your ideal type of client, and that's okay because what you're *really* looking for are people who can connect you with other people who are your ideal type of client. You're not looking for clients; you're looking for connectors.

When you're networking, you're looking for strategic referral partners. Your best referrals might not happen on the day of your networking meetings, but over time. Look at this as a long-term marketing strategy; you'll see the full results typically over the three to six months after you start networking consistently.

Go into your networking event with a list of your top ten ideal strategic referral partners in mind. This doesn't have to be a list of individual people who will be attending; it can be a list of the top ten industries or roles or different professions that you want to connect with. Your ideal strategic partners serve the same ideal client you do, just in different ways or with different products or services.

When I first started my coaching business, my marketing budget was almost nonexistent. I knew you had to "spend money to make money," but I had very little to spend. With networking, back then, it cost less than a dollar a day to join a local Business Network International (BNI) chapter. So I did. In the early days of my coaching business, I helped small-business owners create more efficient businesses so they could love what they were doing and have a great lifestyle. Some of my best strategic referral partners included a real estate agent, an IT company, an estate planning attorney, massage therapist, website designer, and bookkeeper.

Who are *your* ideal strategic partners? List or describe them here.

Top Ten Strategic Partners	
1.	6.
2.	7.
3.	8.
4.	9.
5.	10.

By consciously cultivating strategic referral partners, you find sources that can send you dozens or even hundreds of clients at once, and consistently over time. Focus on building these relationships deep so your networking activity is only the beginning of a long-term strategic referral partnership.

The One-on-One Meeting

There are so many different formats and venues for networking, it's almost impossible to cover them all in a single book! You've got opportunities at chamber of commerce events, organizations like BNI that hold regular networking meetings, online networking and mastermind groups, informal local meetups, and more.

While networking meetings themselves, regardless of the venue and format, can be beneficial in educating potential partners about who your ideal client is and what your perfect referral looks like, your main objective is to arrange a one-on-one meeting with your strategic referral partners *outside* of the general networking meetings. This could be a lunch or dinner meeting during a break in the event program, or a video call after the general networking meeting. Either way, your first step is to connect with these strategic individuals, one by one, and have intentional meetings so that you can strategize on creating a list of specific referrals.

Once you've established someone as a strategic partner and have established a relationship with them, rule number one is do *not* make small talk in these one-on-one meetings. This isn't pleasantries about the weather; it's business. Keep your meeting focused, simple, and guided by the goal that you each will walk away from that one-on-one meeting with introductions that you each will make for specific referrals.

The real magic of networking doesn't come from mingling with the crowd, but from focused meetings where you sit down with somebody and you each get super clear on each other's offer. Then you each open up your contacts book to make a list of who you can refer to each other.

The Magic of Strategic Referrals

To generate the magic of strategic, intentional referrals, you'll need an agenda for your one-on-one meeting with your referral partner. Prepare in advance by adapting my sample agenda to your situation.

- Ten minutes to meet and greet.
- One hour (thirty minutes for each of you) to share specifics about a perfect referral:
  — Share the challenges your ideal client struggles with.
  — Share the transformative result they most want to achieve.
  — Show how each of those things impacts their life.

— Articulate who you want to work with that typically experiences these challenges and wants these results.
— Describe the characteristics of your ideal client.
— Share one or two success stories (or use your own until you have others to add in).
— Specifically ask, "Who do you know that fits this description?"
— Wait for your referral partner to answer, and then have them get out their phone or contact list to identify *exactly* who they know that's a good fit for you.
— Make a list of names of people they know.

- Twenty minutes to strategize together exactly how you will make introductions and pass these referrals to each other (via email, setting up a group lunch, etc.) and other next steps.

The end result you're aiming for is to identify a list of specific names in each other's contact lists who will benefit from a referral. And the best way to pass the referral is usually for the referring partner to reach out to the prospect prior to introductions, explain why they believe the referral is a good thing for the prospect, and directly introduce the other partner. You could do this via a video call or even in person, but email works too (and has fewer scheduling complications).

To help with this part of the process, give your strategic referral partners a simple, pre-written email message template they can use to make writing introduction emails fast and painless. The one we share with our clients looks like this:

Subject Line: {name} meet {name}

Hi {name}, I'd like to introduce you to a colleague of mine, {referral partner name} because {insert why you want them to meet}.

Hi {referral partner name}. I want you to meet my friend {name} because {insert why you want them to meet}.

Let me know if I can do anything else. I'll let you take it from here!

{Your signature}

The Seven Mistakes of the Networking Newbie

Here are a few things to avoid that often prevent entrepreneurs from successful networking. By eliminating these from your networking activities, you'll feel more natural and produce far better results.

Business cards. Do you take business cards with you to in-person networking functions, or carry them around in your purse, bag, or briefcase everywhere you go just in case you bump into a potential client or referral partner? Stop! Business cards don't prompt action. At best, they'll spend the next six months at the bottom of somebody else's purse, bag or briefcase. At worst, they won't even get recycled. Instead, say, "Gosh, I'm sorry. I don't have any business cards. Can I get yours and I'll get in touch with you?" That way *you* are in control of the follow-up so you're not left waiting and hoping for them to contact you.

Socializing. Don't talk to anyone and everyone about anything and everything when you're networking! These mixers and meetings are for your business, so keep them professional with the goal of scheduling a one-on-one meeting. (If you're making friends along the way and want to chitchat, arrange to do that on a separate date *after* your referral meetings!)

Drive-by referrals. Getting an email from a coach who says, "Hi! So-and-so told me to reach out to you because you can really benefit from what I offer..." is... well, it's a little weird. Be sure that your strategic referral partners have discussed the referral with the person before passing them to you! Ideally, have your referral partner introduce you to each other so they can transfer the trust they've built with the prospect and you don't need to make the first contact.

Skills focus. If you get too much into the details of your coaching skill set (what's included in your packages, how many certifications you have, etc.), instead of focusing on the challenges your ideal clients experience and the results they're looking for, your potential referral partners won't get a good sense of *who* they can refer to you.

Mystery business cards. When you dig out a handful of business cards that people gave you at an event, do you remember which card is whose and what you discussed with each of those people? I know I don't! So when someone hands you their business card, make a quick note on the back of the most important things to remember about them and the action you need to take.

No networking follow-up. When you come home with a bunch of business cards, or you stand up from your computer with a bunch of new names and email addresses, it's all too easy to let them sit without getting around to following up with each of them. But when you set up a streamlined referral request process (and automate it) *before* you attend a networking function, you make prompting those referrals effortless and effective. So create an email autoresponder in advance, and as soon as you get your first strategic referral partners, it will fire up to bring in those referrals—while you're basking in the celebration.

No referral follow-up. When a referral partner leverages their trust with their audience and passes referrals to you, it's very helpful for them to know if the referral became a client or not. If you let them know how it went, then they're in a better position to send you more or better referrals the next time! But if they have no idea what happened to their referrals, they might assume that nothing happened at all, which often leads to them not sending any more your way.

Smart Virtual Networking

Because of the way our world has evolved to expect and demand online accessibility and interaction, we coaches have to be ready to network just as effectively in a virtual setting as in a conference hall or a local in-person meeting. No problem! Here are my top tips for smart virtual networking.

Keep it small. Just keep it to you and a handful of other referral partners. When you're meeting online, it can be much easier to focus and support each other with weekly meetings of a small group than to make it through a monthly meeting with ten times as many people! (Large groups aren't inherently bad; they just need to be carefully organized. Being part of both larger and smaller virtual groups can be beneficial.)

Use social networks. Go to the top platform where your ideal clients hang out, identify two or three people who seem like ideal prospects that you'd like to collaborate with, and build relationships with them by commenting on their posts, asking them an interesting question, and so on.

Text (SMS). We've been doing it for so long now in our personal lives that texting has become an intimate and friendly way to communicate. Start using text messaging for your business networking and referral sourcing too. The more informal connections via texting can help cultivate relationships and deepen the trust on a more personal level with your strategic referral partners.

Stay professional. When you're used to working from home in your comfy clothes, it's easy to let your video call standards slip! Everybody who has kids or pets at home while they work sometimes gets interrupted by them, and that's okay as long as it's not the norm. But aside from that unavoidable exception, keep your background tidy and your room well lit with no background noise to create a sense of calm, clarity, and capability. Position your webcam at eye level and invest in a simple light ring.

Name yourself. When you're on a video call, use your full name plus your title or your company name so that people can instantly connect you with your work. For example, "Melinda - The Coaches Console" or "Melinda: Coaching business coach" are a lot more intriguing than just "Melinda."

Follow up. Being intentional is a golden rule not only for virtual networking but for all kinds of networking (and for life in general). So be intentional about your goal of getting and sharing new client referrals, and prepare a follow-up email you'll send to the participants from your virtual networking events to recap the conversation and share contact information.

Above all, relax! Networking is supposed to be fun. (If you don't love it, then at the very least it's supposed to be effective and pain-free.) Everybody you're talking to is a human being whose work you may want to support, and who may be able to support your success too.

Favorite Frames

Take a moment to digest what you've just read. Process what you've taken in so you can make room for even more. Below are some of my favorite frames to recap some of the key points in this chapter.

- You're not looking for clients; you're looking for connectors.

- Leveraging strategic referral partners produces the biggest result with the least effort.
- The magic happens in the one-on-one meeting.
- Prepare a meeting agenda to guide you (or just use mine!)

Feel free to add your own favorite frames in the space below!

Chapter 12
GETTING YOUR MIND RIGHT

Examining Your Relationship with Money

Before we dive deeper into how your coaching business can attract and enroll more new clients, we need to check something:

What's your mindset around making money?

At our live events, I often share teachings about the difference between the *external* work of money and the *internal* work of money that every business owner needs to do for financial success. The external work consists of things like knowing and understanding your crucial financials (budgets, cash flows, reports), mastering the enrollment conversation, and overcoming objections. The internal work is all about understanding how you think and feel about money in your business and in your life, and adopting an internal mindset of abundance and flow that empowers you to make strong, wise decisions about the external matters.

To help with the internal work, I sometimes lead our event attendees through a money meditation that I learned from my money mentor, Barbara Stanny Huson. I met Barbara when I was not in a good place financially, and she changed my entire universe around money!

I had created success early on in my business, but money was something I had struggled with sporadically in my life. I was never so broke that I couldn't afford to eat and pay rent, but I'd struggled to create cash flow at times. With a preacher and a teacher as parents, although we were financially "okay" and they created a wonderful family and household, there was always a sense of scarcity around money. I had an awesome childhood while also being very aware that "money doesn't grow on trees" as Mom used to say.

After becoming an entrepreneur, I got myself into significant financial trouble at one point. I let my lifestyle outpace my income and found myself $40,000 in debt. You might as well have added another zero or two for how monstrous it felt. (Now you know why my dad told me to get a job.) I ignored it for a while, hoping it wasn't real or would just go away. (Of course, it didn't!) When I met Barbara at a program I was participating in and heard her talk about money mindset in her book *Overcoming Underearning*, it made all the difference in how I experienced money personally and as an early entrepreneur. And yes, I did get myself out of debt—without having to get a job—and can now say that I'm debt-free and living from a place of abundance.

Exploring Your Money Mindset Meditation

Even if your mind is already in a good place around money or you're financially successful in your coaching business, the following exercise is beneficial at all business phases and at all levels of financial success. I find it particularly helpful when you're first getting started in business, struggling with having conversations about money, or finding it difficult to make money consistently. This is an exercise I still do regularly to make sure villains don't creep back in. Before you complete these two statements, place your hand on your heart and take a slow, deep breath, then exhale; repeat a few times before you begin to write. Grab a pen or pull up an empty screen, and "fill in the blanks" for the following statements with as many responses as come naturally to you. Don't overthink this; just answer with the authentic thoughts that come into your mind.

- I want to increase my income because…
      {put your answer here}
      {put another answer here}
      {keep going until you run out of answers}

- I'd love to make more money, but…
      {put your answer here}
      {put another answer here}
      {keep going until you run out of answers}

Your answers to the first statement determine your motivation: why increasing your income is important to you. Your *why* is your beacon, guiding your business to achieve your grandest goals. When you have that lighting your path, it's no longer about money. The money is only a means to an end!

Your answers to the second statement reveal your beliefs about what you think you "should" do or "have" to do: who you feel you need to be, and what you believe you need to have before you can make more money. They also reveal the excuses and reasons you use to justify you're not making more money (and, by the way, "I don't know how" is the only legit reason because no one ever taught you).

All these reasons we conjure up as to why we can't do it, no matter how convincing they might seem, are fabrications based on fear instead of fact. It's just our villains creeping in. And I can prove it, because for every reason you might have listed, I can show you several coaches who were in a similar situation and still grew their income!

Take a look through your list of reasons for the second statement. Now change "but..." to "and..." and then write the opposite of that statement in a new list. So if you wrote, "I'd love to make more money, *but* I don't think anyone will pay me higher rates...," you now write in your new list, "I'd love to make more money, *and* my ideal clients are happy to pay a rate that's based on the value of their transformation."

Go through your whole list, writing an opposite "and..." sentence for each item. Now save that final list and put it somewhere you'll see it often! This is the money mindset you want to cultivate so that you can experience ease, abundance, and overflow.

Mirroring and Reflection

One of the things I personally believe is that we mirror to one another parts of ourselves that are similar. Whatever fearful thoughts and limiting beliefs I possess, whatever courage and confidence I have, they'll be reflected back to me in those who are attracted to me, because like attracts like. I actually learned this concept in a training program for yoga teachers, but I saw immediately how I could apply it to benefit my coaching clients and my coaching business!

The Universe guides us into alignment with people who are sufficiently similar, in one way or another, to be able to mirror back to us our needs, our pains, our pleasures and our sacred selves. So our relationships with others, both in our personal lives and in our coaching practices, reflect and magnify who we are. This is one of the beliefs that inspires me to continuously work on self-care and self-improvement, because if I work to free myself of doubts, fears, and stresses, then my clients will begin to reflect that freedom back at me, freeing themselves in the process.

It's why Marianne Williamson's quote from *A Return to Love* was my source of inspiration when I started my coaching business:

Our deepest fear is not that we are inadequate. Our deepest fear is that we are powerful beyond measure. It is our light, not our darkness that most frightens us.... And as we let our own light shine, we unconsciously give others permission to do the same.

The same is true when you're sitting down to have an enrollment conversation with a potential client (or standing on stage to present an offer to a room full of people). If you bring your fears and doubts about money to the enrollment conversation, the person sitting across from you will have *and mirror* those same challenges and struggles, often making it a difficult conversation. Because you're mirroring them too, your prospect's fears trigger your own fears and doubts. It's hard to facilitate a conversation from that triggered place, and it quickly becomes a vicious downward spiral that rarely ends with signing up a new client.

However, when you can work with your coach, mentor, or community, and you can address and reframe your own limiting beliefs around money, then when you show up to an enrollment conversation, you're not triggered, there is no self-judgment, and you can hold space as a confident coach and facilitate a transformational dialogue for your potential client. The work starts with you: only *after* getting your mind right do you work on your enrollment process.

Favorite Frames

Take a moment to digest what you've just read. Process what you've taken in so you can make room for even more. Below are some of my favorite frames to recap some of the key points in this chapter.

- All these reasons we conjure up as to why we can't make more money, no matter how convincing they might seem, are fabrications based on fear instead of fact. It's just our villains creeping in.

- If I work to free myself of doubts, fears, and stresses, then my clients will begin to reflect that freedom back at me, freeing themselves in the process.

- Don't bring your own fears and doubts about money to the enrollment conversation.

Feel free to add your own favorite frames in the space below!

Chapter 13
THE COACH APPROACH
TO ENROLLMENT

What Enrolling Is
(and What It Isn't)

Now that we've got your money mindset right, we can begin to approach the topic of enrolling clients.

First, an important clarification: An enrollment conversation is *not* just a matter of delivering great coaching and hoping you'll get hired to do it some more. (That's the hardest way to approach enrollment!)

Your enrollment conversation should focus on the three Cs of clarity, commitment, and choices. If someone is not clear, is not committed, or does not understand the choices before them, they can't make a buying decision and they'll have never-ending "yeah, but" thoughts and objections. A confused mind never buys.

To convert the right prospects into clients, we need to use our coaching skills to create *clarity*. Your prospect must first be clear on the negative impact of their current, urgent challenges on their lives. This will help them prioritize making changes. Then your prospect must be clear on the results and their positive impact should they choose to make changes in their life. This will help them value what's possible. When they can clearly articulate the results *and* the positive impact those results will have on their life, then they can consider the idea of moving forward with you as their coach and guide.

Once clarity exists, then the conversation becomes a coaching dialogue for you to help them determine the level of *commitment* to making changes. A committed prospect that is prioritizing changes and sees the value of the results is in a position to say, "Yes, let's get started."

When the prospect can articulate the value of the positive impact the results will have on their life, and has a high commitment level, then they can begin to see how your coaching and services can be the vessel to help them get there. Then all that's left is making simple *choices*. This part is about the logistics, such as the coaching package option that's the best fit, or their preferred payment option.

Time after time, I've seen coaches at all levels of experience make the same mistake that only makes enrolling harder—they try to sell the coaching. If you hate selling, then there's a good chance you're doing this too. And you're probably leaving a lot of opportunities (and a lot of money) on the table because of it. Some of those conversations with prospects could have ended with you signing up a new client, if you'd only focused on selling the right thing!

So if coaching is not the right thing to sell, what is?

Don't Sell the Boat

This is a marketing concept I learned so long ago and have seen reinforced by so many in the industry that I'm not even sure where it originated, but I've since adapted it as follows.

When you first encounter your potential clients, they live in a place called "Pain Island." They're struggling with challenges, overwhelmed, stressed, and often at their wits' end. Their fears and struggles keep them awake at night.

That alternative world they're wishing for is their "Pleasure Island." It's their dreams, their desires, their goals—the end results that they most want for themselves. And the only thing they need is... a boat.

PAIN ISLAND & PLEASURE ISLAND

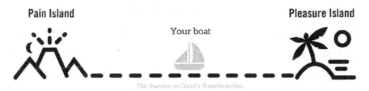

Pain Island and Pleasure Island: Your coaching is the boat that gets clients to where they want to be

Your ideal clients desperately want to be on Pleasure Island. But to cross the space in between Pain Island and Pleasure Island, they need guidance, a way to get from one island to the other. Clearly, what they *need* is a boat (your services, coaching packages, programs, and offers). But what they *want* is Pleasure Island.

Imagine you show up on Pain Island, and you put up two signs on the main street. Sign A says, "Boat trip tickets $10." Sign B says, "Enjoy Paradise: tickets $100." Which sign do you think will have the bigger line of people wanting to get a ticket?

The people on Pain Island don't much care about a boat trip; they just want to get to Pleasure Island. Sure, they need the boat to do that, but the service and the journey are not the focus of their desire. The *destination* is. And the clearer the results are and the more those results bring an end to their struggles and fulfill their urgent needs, the better the value they can see in making the commitment and investing in that transformation.

So don't sell the boat. Don't talk up your coaching services initially; just mention that's what you do (use your "What I do" message from Chapter 7). Paint a picture of the transformations you offer so that you can engage prospects in a dialogue and understand their level of commitment before you take things further.

PAIN ISLAND & PLEASURE ISLAND

Pain Island and Pleasure Island:
Don't sell the boat; sell the destination!

Take a look at the previous image and join me in a quick exercise.

1. Under the image of Pain Island, list three of the most common and most urgent challenges that your ideal type of client struggles with. What keeps them up at night?

2. Now do the same for results under the image of Pleasure Island. If your ideal clients could wave a magic wand and get an instant transformation, what would they wish for? What results do they want the most?

Your coaching services will take your clients from Point A to Point B if they're committed to getting there. So once we know they're interested and committed, then we can start describing the journey and the coaching. (By the way, the clearer your description of Pain Island and Pleasure Island, the better defined your niche is.)

The Ten-Part Outline for Easy Enrollment

To make enrollment conversations easier, use the ten talking points I'm about to share. This isn't intended to be used as a script, but rather more of a checklist to make sure you include the vital elements so it can be an effective dialogue that has coaching integrated throughout.

1. **Conversation Starter:** Ask your prospect why they chose to have this session with you. Their answer helps to identify their top challenges and desired transformation (or their biggest struggles they want to end) so that you can guide the conversation to focus on getting results.

2. **Clarity and Commitment:** Ask about their experience of Pain Island, their vision of Pleasure Island, and the level of their commitment to making change. Can they articulate to you all the ways their current challenges are negatively impacting their life? When they can, this helps to create *priority* for them to make a change. Can they describe to you, in full clarity, the positive impact the results will

have on their life? When they can, you know they see the *value* of taking the journey with you as their coach. Now ask them, "On a scale of 1 to 10, how committed are you to going for these results in your life?" If they say 5 or lower, they aren't committed enough to invest in themselves yet, so politely end the conversation and send them off with a value-based parting gift (like an article or lead magnet). If they're a 10, sign them up! And if they're between 6 and 9, ask, "What would it take for you to be a 10?" Their answers to this question are their objections; often with coaching you can support them to identify potential

3. **Permission:** Make the transition to talking about your services and packages by asking your prospect if they want to know more about how people like them have achieved those same results. Now you have an engaged, curious listener.

4. **A Small Yes:** People have a knee-jerk tendency to say no to *anything*, because refusing seems less risky than agreeing. To prime their mindset for positivity, ask questions throughout the conversation that are easy to say yes to (e.g., "Would getting these results make a big positive change in your life?" or "Can you see how this could help?")

5. **Coaching Agreement:** Use your coaching agreement as a tool to help you explain how the coaching works, convey expectations, list the packages and pricing options, and share the payment options. Your coaching agreement should not be an afterthought or a housekeeping item that you bring up only after someone says yes to hiring you! It's a powerful tool, so bring it to every enrollment conversation.

6. **Result-Based Guarantee:** Be clear about the conditions, including the length of the guarantee period and the fact that your clients have to show up and do the work to be eligible for a refund.

7. **Reflect:** Use your coaching skills and language to repeat back to your prospect the value of the results they articulated to you and the package and options they've expressed interest in the most. This adds another layer of clarity for stronger commitment.

8. **Confirm:** Ask them if they're ready to achieve their desired transformation through that package, with those pricing and payment options. Don't go into all the details again; just check in with them that they're ready to go ahead and start getting the results they've described.

9. **Celebrate:** Remember, your prospect didn't say yes to your *coaching*. They said yes to *themselves*! That's often monumental for most people. Just like

with any coaching client, when they accomplish a significant milestone, it needs to be celebrated. Outrageously acknowledge (in your own style of course) the huge step your new client has just made, validate their decision, and celebrate their commitment to transforming their life!

10. **Onboard:** Now you can collect your new client's signature on your coaching agreement, accept their first payment, roll out the red carpet, and start them on their journey of transformation.

The Four Most Common Enrollment Objections

Good news! The coach approach is ideal for helping you resolve enrollment objections with ease and grace. You're going to bring all of your coaching skills to whatever objections your prospects raise.

Most people despise objections because they interpret them as a moment of failure. I love objections (seriously) because it's a moment for coaching toward deeper clarity. The more objections they have, the more coaching I get to do, and the clearer the prospect gets.

To overcome objections, the first thing you need to know is that *the objection your prospect says out loud is not their real objection.*

Here are the four most common objections you'll hear in enrollment conversations, and what's *really* going on, along with what to do about them:

1. **Money:** "I can't afford it." It's never a money issue; it's that they can't see the value. If this objection comes up, go back and make sure the prospect has a clear picture of their end results and the positive impact those results will have on their lives.

2. **Time:** "I don't have time." We never have time for the things that we don't prioritize! It's never a time issue; it's a priority issue. If this objection comes up, ask the prospect what their real top priorities are.

3. **Spouse:** "I need to talk to my spouse first." This is a common objection because so many partners and families discuss big commitments with each other before making a final decision. (It's also common as a way to procrastinate, allowing your prospect to avoid facing their challenges and the need to act on them.) Don't let them throw their partner under the bus. Have them assume for a moment that their spouse supports them 100 percent then ask them what their level of commitment to take action and move forward is. Clarify their package and pricing preferences before they have that conversation with their spouse. You can also provide great coaching for the prospect in how to talk with

their partner about the decision so they approach it from a place of wanting support rather than needing permission. Be sure to set a date and time for the follow-up conversation no matter what decision is made.

4. **Fear and Self-Doubt:** "I don't think I can make it work." What your prospect really means is that they don't trust themselves to get results. They may have tried another coach or program before without making much progress. Or life may have gotten in the way and they didn't complete things in the past. So remind them of the ways you'll support them to move toward their desired transformation, and ask them what they'll do differently to prioritize their commitment to taking action.

Right now, let's take a more detailed look at how to resolve the most common objection of all: the money objection.

Overcoming the Money Objection

The money objection is most likely the one you'll hear the most, so I'll go deeper on this one to ensure you know exactly how to resolve it.

The one thing you have to constantly remind yourself of when you hear an objection that focuses on the money is that *it's not about the money*! Your prospect *thinks* it is, and that's why you're hearing, "How much? That's too expensive!" or "I can't pay that much," or "I just can't afford it right now." But in reality, the money itself is not the issue. Your price is not the problem. Therefore, addressing the money will never, ever resolve the objection! It only leads to defensiveness for both parties. Now you're in convincing mode—blech!

Even if you set up a monthly payment plan or delay their first payment, give a 10 percent discount, or offer any other solution you can think of that relates to pricing and payment options, it won't solve your prospect's core problem. They'll just say, "Yeah, but..." and then there'll be endless reasons why they can't afford that either.

So don't spend your time and energy talking about the money. Remember, it's not a *money* issue; it's an *I don't see the value* issue. Focus on the root of the objection and make sure they can see and articulate the value of the transformation they'll experience as a result of working with you. Can they paint a clear picture of the positive impact their results will have on their lives when the results become a reality? When your prospect isn't clear about the end result, they will remain skeptical about the value. They'll never invest their money in something they don't see the value of.

I then like to use what I call the "Acknowledge and Redirect" coach approach to overcome their objections. When your prospect brings up the money objection (or any objection), first acknowledge them so they feel seen and heard ("I totally hear you"), and then redirect them ("Before we get to that, let me ask you this…"). Take your prospect back to their vision of Pleasure Island so they can get crystal clear on their future life, their goals, the transformation they want, and the positive impact it will have on them and on the world. When they realize the value and they're ready to commit, *then* you can discuss their options around money.

Favorite Frames

Take a moment to digest what you've just read. Process what you've taken in so you can make room for even more. Below are some of my favorite frames to recap some of the key points in this chapter.

- Enrollment requires the three Cs: clarity, commitment, and choices.
- Identify your ideal client's Pain Island and Pleasure Island.
- Don't sell the boat! Sell the destination—the results.
- The objection your prospect says out loud is not their real objection.
- It's *never* about money!

Feel free to add your own favorite frames in the space below!

Chapter 14
BUILDING BALANCE

Your Business Begins with You

Everyone knows the scenario flight attendants describe as they are going through their safety presentation before taking off. They tell you that in an emergency, you must put on your own oxygen mask first before assisting the person next to you. As a woman, a spouse, a parent, a coach, I still feel even after all the years of traveling that I've done that that instruction is a bit counterintuitive. But logically, it makes sense. If I don't take care of myself first, then I won't even be around to assist anybody else. The same is true in your business.

Everything you've read so far in this book will work at maximum effectiveness only if you take care of yourself as well as taking care of business—because your business begins with you.

Self-care is one of the most important and essential tasks for every entrepreneur and business owner. It's something I prioritize every day for my business. If I'm not taking care of myself, then I will be *less* myself. I want to bring *all* of me to my business, not sputtering on fumes. I believe that I, my husband, my family, my business, my clients, and my community deserve better than that.

If you don't bring your total self to your business, you'll struggle more to make less progress, and sooner or later the overwhelm will defeat you. It's the recipe for burnout. You'll run out of time, energy, passion and money before you create sustainable, consistent success. That's when it starts feeling like you're pushing a boulder uphill, and even worse when you start doubting your skills, your calling, and yourself.

Earlier in this book I showed you how balancing our masculine and feminine aspects in business generates the greatest success. And I'm sure you've heard of (and struggled to achieve) that magical thing called "work-life balance." But let me share a secret with you: I actually dislike the word *balance* in a coaching context. Ever since I started as a coach, the misuse and misperception of that word has been like fingernails on a chalkboard for me! I firmly believe there's no such thing as achieving balance unless you can hit pause on the Universe.

Let's be clear about what balance is and isn't before we dig any deeper.

- Balance is *not* something you have; it's something you experience.

- Balance is *not* a one-and-done thing; it's an ongoing, never-ending process.

- Balance is *not* a sign of inherent perfection; it's a side effect of continuous, intentional alignment.

- Balance is *not* about staying still; it's about shifting continuously in response to feedback.

Everything is in continuous movement and flow, and that flow is the source of all balance, all life, and all existence. So if you insist on trying to freeze it all in one place of perfection or "just right," you're asking the entire Universe to act against its nature. (Please, do not try this at home.)

In order to bring your total self to your business, it's important to define who you need to become in order to have a successful coaching business. There are no right or wrong answers, by the way. You define your success on your own terms, and only you can say what you feel you need or who you need to be to achieve it. But knowing this answer helps to understand how you need to show up in your business and the level of self-care you need so you can maintain a healthy balance.

My own answer to that question is that I'm not only interested in owning a successful coaching business. I want a successful and profitable coaching business that *also* creates a successful lifestyle beyond my wildest dreams *and* lets me make a positive impact in this world through my work, services, and leadership, leaving it better than when I found it. Oh, *and*, I want to get paid. A lot. *And* I want to love my work. *And...* (I'll stop there. As I'm sure you can see, we all have multiple concepts of meaning, fulfillment, and legacy wrapped up in the way we view our coaching businesses.)

Your answer to this question will change over time. In fact, if you had asked me the same question a couple of decades ago, I would have told you with absolute certainty that I didn't want a coaching business, or any business of my own at all. I never imagined myself as an entrepreneur.

Creating a successful business (or doing anything successful in life) begins with you: It's who you are and how you show up in the world, in your life, and in your business. The feelings you have drive the thoughts you think. The more you think the thoughts, the more they turn into actions. And as you take action, those feelings and thoughts become things.

Your inner self drives your perspective, your ability to be profoundly comfortable with the discomfort of being an entrepreneur, your creative thinking, decision-making, and more. And to attract your ideal clients to your business, you first have to "get yourself right" before you can build powerful, effective relationships with others. The better your inner world matches your outer world, the greater flow you experience.

Rituals

Taking care of yourself before taking care of business makes perfect sense, so prioritize self-care and spiritual well-being to prepare yourself for even greater success in your business.

These, in no particular order, are a few of the rituals I do regularly:

- **Gratitude** — Either writing gratitudes in my journal or saying them out loud.

- **Meditation** — To give space to stress, thoughts, or emotions so they can have room to be expressed, felt, and moved through without getting stuck.

- **Breathwork** — I've found this the quickest and easiest way to change a situation, or transform entire feelings and emotions, and reconnect with myself.

- **Movement** — Whether it's yoga or Qoya or a quick dance break, regularly moving my body throughout the day helps me get out of my head and into my body, so I can fully process experiences and be present in the moment.

- **Self-Care** — I might have a massage, acupuncture, a manicure, or a treatment with a chiropractor, for example, to help me stay healthy, relaxed, and ready to kick ass. Or it can be as simple as reading a book, taking a nap, or having lunch with a close friend.

- **Celebrations** — Whether it's "bragging" about my latest accomplishments in my journal, or celebrating the successes of my clients, acknowl-edging our achievements makes us more confident and capable to tackle our next steps and achieve even more. And by bragging, I don't mean boasting or being arrogant to make others feel "less than." To brag is simply to shine the spotlight on yourself and to unapologetically tell the truth about your own celebrations and accomplishments.

- **Time in Nature** — This can be taking a walk, eat-ing lunch outdoors, or just sitting down in nature and taking time to really sense the world around me. No matter what I'm doing, taking it out into nature sharpens my senses and refreshes my sense of unity and connection with the Universe.

I could go on and on, as I have many more acts of self-care that I integrate regularly in my daily life and business. But you get the idea. You might already have your own rituals that keep you centered in spirit. If you don't, or you're open to adding more, pick one or two that appeal to you from the previous list and give them a try for a week or two to see how they positively impact your business success!

The True Meaning of "Always do Your Best"

For years, I used to strive for perfection in everything, not because I wanted to except, but because I desperately feared failing and looking bad. I've loved snow skiing since I was eleven years old—I mean, seriously, my license plate says SKI GDSS (Ski Goddess). In hindsight, I realized that throughout my teenage years and into my mid-20s, I would take only the slopes that I *knew* I wouldn't fall on and that I'd look good going down (which seems so silly now, but it's the truth). I missed out on a lot of adventures because I played it super safe. My friends were skiing harder trails, which meant fewer people, shorter lift lines, and prettier parts of the mountain with gorgeous views, not to mention the better snow and fresh powder.

It wasn't until after my divorce that I started really learning how to live *my* life. I was skiing in Banff with some friends who skied together a lot. One day during après-ski (a.k.a. happy hour), they were talking about the incredible places they skied that day, the fresh powder they found, and the amazing fun they had. I finally had enough; I didn't want to just hear about these stories, I wanted to *live* them for myself! So I asked if I could ski with them the next day. I vowed to myself that wherever they went, I would go. And I would just follow in their tracks and watch them and emulate them. Whatever they did, I would do. I knew that if I got into trouble, they'd be there to help me.

There was no backing out then. So the next day, I joined them and we headed out through the trees, over rocks, down extremely steep slopes I was nervous and quite petrified. But I just kept telling myself, "Do what they do, stay in their tracks, and you can do it too, Melinda"…and I did!

That was when I really understood that "always do your best" doesn't mean striving to be perfect. Your best today may not look like your best yesterday or even what it will look like tomorrow. But today, do your best. Did I fall down on that mountain? Yes, more than I ever had in my life. Did I get stuck? You bet I did; my friends had to come and help me out. Was I scared? Yes, I was freaking terrified at times. It was messy and I made mistakes, but I did my best. My commitment and my courage was just one degree louder than my fear, and that's all it took.

"You Get What You Tolerate."

When I first met my father-in-law, he shared this concept with me. It was the first time I'd heard it, and it hit me like a ton of bricks. It was both disheartening and empowering at the same time. The control freak in me loved the idea, because it meant if there was something I was tolerating, I could change it! But on the flip side, if there was something I was tolerating, I couldn't blame that on some external factor; I had to do something about it myself if I wanted it to change.

My husband and I still live our lives by this mantra every day. We're always asking, "What am I tolerating?" so that our answers give us the opportunity to respond, either by doing something about it or by intentionally deciding we're not ready to change it yet and focusing our attention on other areas.

What are you tolerating in your business? Are you okay with that toleration, or is it time to change?

Including Spirit

Before beginning with business, I think it's important to include Spirit. We are simultaneously spiritual beings having a human experience *and* human beings having a spiritual experience.

For anything to be successful (business, family, relationship, etc.), we must bring all of ourselves to that thing, both our human selves and our spiritual selves, so we can tap into the magic and power of both to create and cultivate success. When we remember we're spiritual beings, we hold to our truth, stay grounded in a higher power, leave room for the magic of the Universe, and realize we don't have to shoulder our burdens alone on our journey.

It doesn't matter what you call that higher power, or how you imagine it to exist. Just acknowledging there's something beyond our human selves that plays a part in our journeys will make a difference in your path to success.

Favorite Frames

Take a moment to digest what you've just read. Process what you've taken in so you can make room for even more. Below are some of my favorite frames to recap some of the key points in this chapter.

- Everything you've read in this book will work only if you take care of yourself as well as taking care of your business.

- The better your inner world matches your outer world, the greater flow you experience.

- Leave room for the magic of the Universe, and realize you don't have to shoulder your burdens alone on your journey.

Feel free to add your own favorite frames in the space below!

Chapter 15
FINDING FLOW

Knowing Your Why

Your reason *why* you coach is the beacon that drives everything in your coaching business. So to succeed, you must be clear about exactly what your *why* is, and keep it always at the front of your mind and at the core of your daily actions and decisions.

If you had asked me back in 2004 why I became a coach, I'd have told you it was pretty simple: I'd just been fired and recently divorced, I was living alone, and I had been doing coaching as a hobby and needed to find a way to support myself financially (because I wasn't about to let anyone else be in charge of my future ever again).

But are any of those reasons for becoming a coach, specifically? Nope! They're just reasons to get a job... and if getting a job were really that simple, I would've gone to the local job ads and started applying for interior design roles because I already had the necessary experience and credentials.

The real reason behind my desire to coach was that I felt called to help others be the best they could be, and coaching came naturally to me. It felt right in a way that no other option did. Coaching lit me up inside. I could have gotten a job in some other field, and I'm sure I would've had a nice enough life, but coaching called to me, and I answered because my *why* would not allow me to keep silent.

In hindsight, I can see the through line of my *why*. Interestingly enough, my *why* was the same when I was an interior designer—only the *how* changed. As an interior designer, I created spaces in which people could be their best and do their best. As a coach, I help people be their best and do their best no matter what space they're in. As a coach to coaches, I help coaches create their best business to help others be their best.

I also love systems, processes, and all forms of organization, and unbeknownst to me, that was the secret of my swift success as a newbie coach. If I was going to put myself out there to find clients, talk to them about what I could offer, and the results that were possible, I had to make sure I could deliver on what I was promising. So I set up systems (pieced together in Word, Excel, Outlook, and QuickBooks at first) that made it much easier for me to manage my business and support my clients, and those systems facilitated the early wins in my coaching career. They also helped me feel more confident and professional right out of the gate.

Within six months of starting my coaching business, I had a full practice, and everything was going really well.

Then I heard a voice that came from "nowhere." Yep, seriously. I was riding in a friend's car one day, and a voice spoke to me. But when I asked my friend if he heard it, he said he didn't hear a thing. It was a voice from within.

Being around God, church, and spirit my whole life, I knew where that voice was coming from, and I knew I had to listen to it. So I pulled a napkin out of the glove box of the car and began writing what I was hearing:

> Enable those who are fulfilling their life's purpose via coaching to do that the best way possible...
>
> Eliminate the burdens and distractions of coaches...
>
> Enable new coaches to begin sooner so they don't have to wait for the money foundation...
>
> Creation of processes for follow-up, marketing, paperwork, organization, client management...

At the time I heard this voice and scribbled down its message, it made *zero* sense to me. After all, I was a new coach just getting started. Was I supposed to coach coaches? What did I know about that? What did that mean, to "eliminate the burdens and distractions of coaches"? Even though I had no clue what it meant, the message continued to tug at me. So I tucked the napkin away on my desk and let it sit for a while.

Remember, at this point I was just six months into start-ing my coaching business. I was still working with Kate as she coached me around my growing business. And because I didn't know much about the coaching industry at that point, I just figured the success I'd already experienced as a new coach and a new entrepreneur was the norm. I thought *all* coaches—heck, all entrepreneurs—first set up the internal and necessary business systems to operate and automate their businesses so they could be freed to coach more and make more money doing what they loved. Silly me!

When I showed Kate how I'd set up and organized my business based on the pile of papers and stacks of folders she'd given me plus my own love of automated systems, she said, "*I want what you've got!*"

And she was even more surprised at my naivety, think-ing that this was just how all coaches did it! So she set me straight: "No Melinda, most coaches don't experience the success you are experiencing. I've been coaching for three years now, and I think it's time you coach me to set up this same type of organization in my business so I can experi-ence that level of success without being overwhelmed and without working so hard."

That conversation really opened my eyes to the typical experiences of coaches. If a coach as skilled and experienced as Kate, who was also a natural at networking and at getting clients, still felt overwhelmed and burdened by the busi-ness side of her practice, then that meant any (every!) coach could benefit from taking my strategic, systematic approach to their back office. Kate gave me a whole new perspective by showing me that most coaches struggle because their efforts are scattered, and they eventually fail because they don't know how to operate their businesses with *less* effort in a *more* strategic and intentional way. In that moment, I began to realize what the napkin meant.

I showed her my napkin and told her the story. And I said to her, "If you need something like what I've created for my business, maybe other coaches need it as well. Maybe we could create something together so we can help other coaches be successful." What I knew for sure was that even though I didn't fully understand *how* the napkin vision would play out, I knew it was bigger than me. This vision was way bigger than one person, so I invited Kate to join me as a business partner in helping create success for other coaches. That was the birth of The Coaches Console.

Kate's mission and passion is to get the world coached. As only two coaches with a finite amount of time, we could coach only so many people. But if we helped other coaches "eliminate the burdens and distractions" of their businesses so they could "live their God-given potential," they could then coach more clients and we could fulfill the vision of getting the world coached.

My *why* became not only to coach and serve others, but also to unburden coaches of *their* overwhelm by helping them implement systems that do a lot of the work for them so that they can concentrate on the coaching work they love and do best.

That napkin hung on the wall in my office as a constant reminder of my *why*. And now, seventeen years later (at the time of writing this book), that single voice (that vision) has turned into a multimillion-dollar business that has impacted thousands of coaches to have thriving coaching businesses around the world. I now know that the newest articulation of my *why* is to help you build a better business so you can be a better coach so we can build a better world.

How do you find your *why*? Here's a simple exercise I call the "stairstep" to your why. Answer these questions:

1. Why did you start your business?
2. Why do you want to _____?

   {insert answer to first step}

3. Why do you want to _____?

   {insert answer to second step}

4. Keep going up the stairs until you can't answer the question anymore.

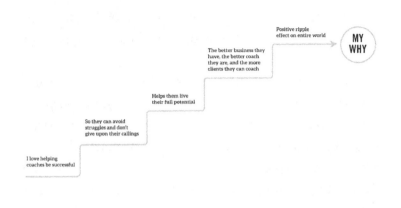

The stairstep to your why: Keep going until you've uncovered your highest motivation!

Giving (and Creating) from our Overflow

So often entrepreneurs push so hard to succeed that they end up running on fumes. But when you're depleted, disconnected, and drained, you don't see clearly and you're not thinking clearly, and that means you're not bringing your greatest skills, talents, and gifts to the business (or project or client).

Is it *possible* to start, run, and manage your business on fumes? Sure, but it comes at a high cost. Taking the head-down, nose-to-the-grindstone approach can negatively impact your health and increase stress. When you're under stress for extended periods of time, it's harder to take wise, decisive action. Everything becomes more difficult and harder to navigate, like the feeling of pushing a boulder uphill.

Instead, by integrating self-care, your body will naturally produce nitric oxide, oxytocin, and other endorphins that are the key to maintaining optimum health, clarity, and creativity so you can bring all the best parts of yourself to serve your passion, your vision, your business, and your clients. This, for me, is at the heart of what I do to have a successful business. I dedicate my time, energy, and resources to use the tools at my disposal along with practicing self-care so I can minimize the stress running through my body. It's a priority and a natural way of living for me, and it makes all the difference in how I show up in my business.

When you take care of yourself—energetically, emotionally, spiritually, creatively, intellectually, and physically— you continuously build up reserves of energy within you, so you'll have more than enough for yourself and more than enough surplus to give to others.

Imagine a pitcher of water. You are the pitcher, and the water is your energy. You pour the water out of the pitcher every day into various cups—relationships, clients, appointments, projects, your business—until it's empty. Then you have to stop and refill it before you can start to give again. This start-stop approach often leaves you running on empty because most people rarely take the time to refill their pitcher. They just keep giving.

Instead, take a bit of time, up front, and fill the pitcher with water until it's full, and then *keep filling* until it's overflowing. Hold the glasses below the pitcher and as you continue to fill it, the water overflows to simultaneously fill every glass. When you fill yourself to overflow and stay connected to the source, your energy is never depleted. You're not exhausted or burned out, and the people around you benefit as you give of your overflow to serve and support them at the same time. Use some of the self-care rituals from the previous chapter, or create your own, to keep yourself filled up.

Favorite Frames

Take a moment to digest what you've just read. Process what you've taken in so you can make room for even more. Below are some of my favorite frames to recap some of the key points in this chapter.

- Follow your *why* like your business depends on it (because it does!).

- Prioritize self-care and well-being to keep your energy flowing so that you always have more to give.

- Bring all the best parts of yourself to serve your passion, your vision, your business, and your clients from a place of overflow.

Feel free to add your own favorite frames in the space below!

THE DEBRIEF

What We've Learned Together

The coaching industry is going through *a new stage of evolution* as the world around us has become increasingly complex and chaotic.

Coaching has evolved *from a nice-to-have luxury to a necessity* that the everyday person is seeking out.

There is a *huge opportunity* for coaches everywhere, in every niche.

As entrepreneurs and as coaches, we are part of the solution. *We* are the leaders people are turning to, to help them navigate their challenges and lives with purpose and create a future they desire.

The trigger for real transformation involves taking a *coach approach* to building and running your business, using your natural gifts and the skills of coaching to create a business advantage.

There are *five business phases* and *seven success structures* that every coaching business must implement for success.

The way in which you *implement and automate* the components of your coaching business's back office makes all the difference between being burdened by your business and being liberated by your business.

Start with the marketing tactic that most *resonates with your natural style* and is aligned with the business phase you're currently in.

The objection your prospect says out loud is *not their real objection*.

When you build *success structures* for yourself as well as for your business, the positive impact on both is undeniable.

Self-care empowers you to *give of your overflow*, bringing your whole self to your business and your clients without ever feeling depleted.

Together, we will build better businesses, become better coaches, and build a better world, by transforming the business of coaching to deliver *transformative results*.

Your Top Takeaways

Use this space like the favorite frames section at the end of every chapter, but take your perspective book-wide to pinpoint your most impactful insights and takeaways. Then write them here for quick reference!

Debrief Q&A

1. **What went well?** — What concepts and practices did you instantly connect with and feel you understood clearly enough to implement in your business?

2. **What didn't go well?** — What sections of the book do you feel you could use additional insight on and resources to help you implement?

3. **What will *you* do differently next time?** — What changes do you intend to implement in your coaching business as a result of what you've read in this book? (Also: When you next pick up this book, which sections will you reread to improve your knowledge and cultivate your capacity for implementation?)

Clarity

Knowing everything you now know about how you can build a better business, to be a better coach, to build a better world, list the top three results that you want to realize with your coaching business.

Result #1: _____

Result #2: _____

Result #3: _____

Now list your top three most important things to focus on so you can move the needle in your business and deliver those transformative results for yourself and your clients.

Priority #1: _____

Priority #2: _____

Priority #3: _____

Do a quick logic check: Will working on the three priorities you just listed help you make your top three results a reality? If not, rethink your top three priorities until they align with your top three results.

Commitment

On a scale of 1 (not at all) to 10 (absolutely), how committed are you to acting on the priorities you listed so that you can create the results you want to see in your business and in your life?

Circle your answer here:

1   2   3   4   5   6   7   8   9   10

If you're lower than a 10, what's stopping you from fully committing to growth and increased success in your coaching business? Note your answers to this question, then refer back to Chapter 2 to understand how your services are a necessity in today's word. Also revisit Chapter 15 to get clarity on your *why* and the passion driving your desire to have your own business.

Choices

To help, guide, and support you in implementing the changes you've identified and prioritized, we've lovingly prepared a stack of valuable content for you. Take a look through the following options and explore the links to detailed information on the ones that interest you the most.

Whether you start with a free downloadable PDF or jump right into a workshop or event, we're here to ease your burdens so you can feel confident in your coaching business success!

ADDITIONAL RESOURCES TO SUPPORT YOU!

GET THE AUDIOBOOK + THE ULTIMATE COACHING BUSINESS SUCCESS TOOL KIT

Receive the free audiobook PLUS our Ultimate Coaching Business Success Tool Kit, a valuable download with a complete checklist and the precise sequence to implement the seven success systems within your business.

→ Download it at **www.confident-coach.com/toolkit**

ATTEND A FREE COACHING BUSINESS SYSTEM WORKSHOP

Ready to roll up your sleeves and start implementing? Attend our free online workshop to go deeper into the ideas in this book and put them into practice.

→ Sign up for free at **www.confident-coach.com/workshop**

JOIN US IN PERSON AT THE BUSINESS OF COACHING LIVE!

Discover how to implement the right success structures for your business to grow and thrive with ease in our three-day intensive training event.

→ Reserve your spot at **www.confident-coach.com/live**

A REQUEST

Thank You for Reading My Book!

I would love hearing what you thought about the book.
Please leave me a helpful review on Amazon!

Thanks so much!
~ Melinda Cohan

ACKNOWLEDGMENTS

Thank you—those words are not strong enough to express the depth of gratitude that I have for...

Dave, the love of my life beyond my wildest dreams, for being my rock. You help me infuse my sparkle into all that I am and all that I do.

Mom, for being my true believer. I'm grateful for the "It's a rare person who can take care of hearts while also taking care of business" plaque you gave me in the early years of the business. It has served as a constant reminder for how I want to show up in business. I'm just sorry you're no longer with us to see this become a reality, but I know you're celebrating with me in Spirit. Dad, for being my hero, becoming my naysayer when I most needed it, and then becoming my greatest motivator to get me into action. Stephanie, my favorite sister, for teaching me to focus on and savor one day at a time. Danielle and Dylan, who inspire me to be the best version of myself.

Kate, my business partner, soul sister, ski buddy, and the Queen of Fun, for your unwavering support and never-ending belief in me. I'll forever cherish that day in Barnes & Noble when you smeared my vision napkin with chocolate mocha and we officially became business partners and birthed The Coaches Console. *Wow*, what a journey. Cosmin, for your gigantic heart, programming genius, and for helping Kate and me, as coaches, figure out what the heck we were doing owning a software company!

My entire team, for being the best guardian angels and best *chosen family* ever! It is a privilege to lead and serve you. I truly could not and would not want to do this great adventure called "business" without you!

My former coaches and mentors...

Kate, for being my first coach. You introduced me to a whole new world, taught me how to be a coach steeped in integrity, and most of all how to embrace my fun. Boa Babes forever! Jean-Pierre LeBlanc, for helping me to discover my inner goddess. Lise Janelle, for reminding me that love has a place in business. Michael Port, who helped us see that we were more than a coaching company...that we were also a software company—duh! Regena Thomashauer, a.k.a. Mama Gena, who created the container for me to discover and live *all* eighty-eight keys of me in this world. Justin Livingston, for your friendship and for sharing your playful genius so we could finally kick over the seven-figure mark! Jeff Walker, for creating the greatest mastermind group and bringing together the most amazing people in the world— what an honor to be part of that *family*. Stu McLaren, you encouraged me through uncertainty, fear and doubt as the phoenix was rising from the ashes. Thank you for being my cheerleader. Danny Iny, for reigniting my vision, passion, and creativity, and for exemplifying all of your core values in the way you lead and serve those around you.

My colleagues courageous enough to write their own books... Thank you for paving the way.

To what I think of as my inner, sacred circle of sisters...

Victoria Labalme, for helping me to stay within the "V" and keep my writing pure and in integrity. Michelle Falzon, for teaching me the power and pace of percolating as a necessary part of every project, especially birthing a book. Margaret Lynch, for encouraging me (actually demanding me!) to speak on her stage and unleashing me to step into my own confidence in greater ways. Annie Hyman Pratt, for teaching me to have massive compassion in all that I do. Ann Wilson, for your encouragement, love, and support when I was a hot mess to keep going or I never would have made it to the point of even writing this book.

To all the PLAT+ mastermind group members...

You help me play a bigger, more meaningful game in business and in life. I am inspired by each of you every day.

My confidants and Sister Goddesses...

Lindsay McKinnon, Beth Baxter Sharman, and Nell Daniel, thank you for our countless brags, desires, swamps, and spring cleans and for reflecting and reminding me of who I truly am and what I'm truly capable of. We are the women we once dared to desire to be. Thank you for helping me to work my tools so I can be the greatest version of the grandest vision of myself.

My students, graduates, and The Coaches Console members, for entrusting me to teach and coach you on your epic business journeys. It is an honor and privilege to be your guide. You are my *why*!

My first readers, Tom Brush, Dr. Melinda Hill, and Dave Cohan. I'm grateful for the specific feedback and insights to help make this book the best version it could be. And for making sure it's inclusive for all coaches no matter their age, gender, race, or culture.

My writing and publishing team...

Sophie Lizard, my writing collaborator. To say I couldn't have done this without you is a massive understatement. Thank you for helping me make sense of all my brain dumps and finding my voice. I knew I had all the pieces, and you helped me put them together! You are a phenomenal writer. Allyson Machate and the team at The Writer's Ally, for making the editing process easy and a blast and for helping this book be more than I could have dreamed it to be! Molly McCowan, my editor. When you submitted your editorial letter after reviewing my first manuscript draft, I was no longer just someone who was writing a book; you taught me what it meant to be a writer. Thank you for your guidance, style, and wisdom. Emily Hitchcock, for creating a cover that elegantly and powerfully captures the essence of the book's message. To the team at Storehouse Media Group, for their help with the countless details necessary to get this book published.

And last but not least, thank you, God; thank you, Goddess; thank you, Universe, for always having my back and dazzling and delighting me every day!

BIBLIOGRAPHY

Campbell, Mikey. "Tim Cook Says Privacy 'One of the Top Issues of the Century.'" AppleInsider. January 29, 2021. https://appleinsider.com/articles/21/01/29/tim-cook-says-privacy-one-of-the-top-issues-of-the-century.

Canfield, Jack, Mark Victor Hansen, and Les Hewitt. *The Power of Focus: How to Hit Your Business, Personal and Financial Targets with Absolute Certainty.* Boca Raton: HCI, 2000.

Chapman, Glenn. "Google Moves Away from Diet of 'Cookies' to Track Users." Yahoo! News. February 6, 2021. https://news.yahoo.com/google-moves-away-diet-cookies-041325414.html.

Chenoweth, Erica, Austin Choi-Fitzpatrick, Jeremy Pressman, Felipe G. Santos, and Jay Ulfelder. "The global pandemic has spawned new forms of activism – and they're flourishing." *Guardian* (US edition). April 20, 2020. https://www.theguardian.com/commentisfree/2020/apr/20/the-global-pandemic-has-spawned-new-forms-of-activism-and-theyre-flourishing.

Collins, Sarah. "Using Pain and Pleasure to Win the Sale." AllBusiness.com. Accessed February 28, 2021. https://www.allbusiness.com/using-pain-and-pleasure-to-win-the-sale-14053742-1.html.

Dahlberg, Tim. "Ali, Frazier and the Fight of the Century 50 Years Later." AP News. March 7, 2021. https://apnews.com/article/muhammad-ali-joe-frazier-fight-of-century-50-years-later-1cec64d531bcca41d6b1fe21cd50c0d8.

Gorton, Gregg E. "Milton Hyland Erickson, 1901–1980." *American Journal of Psychiatry* 162, no. 7 (July 2005): 1255. https://doi.org/10.1176/appi.ajp.162.7.1255.

IBISWorld. "Business Coaching Industry in the US - Market Research Report." Updated January 25, 2021. https://www.ibisworld.com/united-states/market-research-reports/business-coaching-industry/.

IBISWorld. "Life Coaches Industry in the US - Market Research Report." Updated August 30, 2020. https://www. ibisworld.com/united-states/market-research-reports/ life-coaches-industry/.

IMDb. "Chariots of Fire (1981)." Accessed May 18, 2021. https://www.imdb.com/title/tt0082158.

International Coaching Federation. *COVID-19 and the Coaching Industry*. Lexington: International Coaching Federation, 2020. Accessed 12 February, 2021. https:// coachingfederation.org/app/uploads/2020/09/FINAL_ ICF_GCS2020_COVIDStudy.pdf

International Coaching Federation. *2020 ICF Global Coaching Study Executive Summary*. Lexington: International Coaching Federation, 2020. Accessed 12 February, 2021. https://coachingfederation.org/ app/uploads/2020/09/FINAL_ICF_GCS2020_ ExecutiveSummary.pdf

Kubu, Cynthia, and Andre Machado. "Why Multitasking Is Bad for You." *Time*. April 20, 2017. https://time.com/4737286/ multitasking-mental-health-stress-texting-depression.

LaRosa, John. "U.S. Personal Coaching Industry Tops $1 Billion, and Growing." MarketResearch.com. February 12, 2018. https://blog.marketresearch.com/us-personal-coaching-industry-tops-1-billion-and-growing.

Leland, Azadeh, Kamran Tavakol, Joel Scholten, Debra Mathis, David Maron, and Simin Bakhshi. "The Role of Dual Tasking in the Assessment of Gait, Cognition and Community

Oelze, Patricia. "How Milton Erickson Revolutionized Modern Therapy." BetterHelp. Updated February 8, 2021. https://www.betterhelp.com/advice/psychologists/how-milton-erickson-revolutionized-modern-therapy.

Online Etymology Dictionary. "Coach." Accessed February 4, 2021. https://www.etymonline.com/word/coach.

Port, Michael. *Book Yourself Solid: The Fastest, Easiest, and Most Reliable System for Getting More Clients Than You Can Handle Even if You Hate Marketing and Selling*. Hoboken: Wiley, 2006.

Sawyer, R. Keith. "Conclusion: The Future of Learning: Grounding Educational Innovation in the Learning Sciences." In *The Cambridge Handbook of the Learning Sciences*. 2nd ed., ed. R. Keith Sawyer, 726–746. Cambridge:

Cambridge University Press, 2014. https://doi.org/10.1017/CBO9781139519526.043.

Stanny, Barbara. *Overcoming Underearning: A Five-Step Plan to a Richer Life*. New York: Collins, 2007.

The Milton H. Erickson Foundation. "Biography of Milton H. Erickson." Accessed May 12, 2021. https://www.erickson-foundation.org/biography/.

Thomashauer, Regena. *Pussy: A Reclamation*. Carlsbad: Hay House, 2016.

Uță, Iulia-Cristina. "How Entrepreneurship Is Changing the World." Brand Minds. November 6, 2018. https://brandminds.live/how_entrepreneurship-is-changing-the-world/.

Wikipedia. "Milton H. Erickson." Accessed February 27, 2021. https://en.wikipedia.org/wiki/Milton_H._Erickson.

Williamson, Marianne. *A Return to Love: Reflections on the Principles of a Course in Miracles*. New York: HarperCollins, 1992.

ABOUT THE AUTHOR

Melinda Cohan is a business coach to coaches. She achieved fast success when she launched her own coaching business, quickly replacing the income from her previous job as a workplace-efficiency interior designer.

In 2004 she started coaching other coaches to grow their businesses, based on a vision she'd scribbled on the back of a napkin to "eliminate the burdens and distractions of coaches" using her expertise in designing systems and processes. She became the co-founder and CEO of The Coaches Console, now a seven-figure software, training, and coaching company that has helped more than fifty thousand coaches create profitable and thriving businesses.

Cohan's work has given her an insider's view of the coaching industry: every kind of coach, every kind of business model, every kind of challenge and solution, every shift in the coaching industry. Now she wants to share her insight with you so you can take the complexity out of your coaching business and turn your passion and talent into profit.

When she isn't coaching, Cohan enjoys the outdoors (especially skiing); going to concerts and football games with her husband, Dave; spending time with her stepchildren, Danielle and Dylan; and creating adventures with her family.